THE MILITARY TO CIVILIAN TRANSITION GUIDE

2011-2012 Edition

A Career Transition Guide for Army, Navy, Air Force, Marine Corps & Coast Guard Personnel

Carl S. Savino and Ronald L. Krannich, Ph.D.

COMPETITIVE EDGE SERVICES INC.
Fairfax Station, Virginia

Employment and Services

This book is made available to you through the generous support of many military-friendly sponsors. Companies identified as employers have immediate job opportunities suitable for transitioning military. They welcome receiving your resume and invite you to visit their websites for additional information on their job opportunities. Other organizations provide important services for you and your family. Please let them know that you are responding to their opportunities listed in *The Military to Civilian Transition Guide*.

Employers

Consulting

- Collins Consulting

Defense

- CACI
- Chenega Technology Services Corporation
- DDL Omni Engineering
- General Dynamics Information Technology
- JB&A
- Lockheed Martin
- L-3 MPRI
- Unisys

Engineering

- Applied Physics Laboratory
- Argon ST

Financial Services

- State Farm Insurance
- Uniformed Services Benefit Association

Government

- Defense Intelligence Agency
- National Security Agency
- Department of Veterans Affairs
- U.S. Department of Health and Human Services, National Institutes of Health

Information Technology

- Advanced Resource Technologies Inc.
- Unisys Corporation

Retail/Services

- Amazon
- ARAMARK
- Sodexo
- Wal-Mart

Telecommunications

- Verizon FNS
- Verizon Wireless

Training/Schools

- DeVry University
- ECPI College of Technology

Transition Services

- Aerotek
- Corporate Gray Online
- IntelligenceCareers.com

Contents

ISBNs: 978-0-9838489-0-5 (13-digit); 0-9838489-0-4 (10 digit)

Acknowledgments: Our ability to provide this book free to all transitioning service members is a direct result of the support of many advertising sponsors. We appreciate the support of these fine organizations and encourage you to take advantage of their transition-related products, services, and career opportunities. You will find information on these sponsors in the front section of this book, including their websites and phone numbers, in the section entitled "Employment and Services." We also wish to thank each branch of the Armed Forces for giving us the opportunity to donate a Corporate Gray Series™ Transition Guide to everyone separating or retiring from active duty. And it is to you—the men and women who have served our nation in peace and war—to whom we dedicate this book. May you have a successful career transition!

verizonwireless

Verizon Wireless is an equal opportunity employer m/f/d/v.

verizonbusiness
We're Verizon Federal Network Systems (FNS) and we're in motion.

DEFENSE INTELLIGENCE AGENCY
UNITED STATES OF AMERICA
DEFENSE INTELLIGENCE AGENCY
Your Intelligence Protecting America
You are passionately patriotic and extraordinarily talented in your field, and you welcome great challenges because of the opportunities they present. You belong at the Defense Intelligence Agency (DIA) – America's premier military intelligence organization dedicated to protecting the country and deterring would-be aggressors. The Department of Defense and the entire Intelligence Community depend upon our people to be elite-in-class, whether they are traveling internationally to collect and analyze information or working in Washington, DC or one of our global locations, to provide scientific, technical, administrative and management support. DIA offers civilians and students the full range of career opportunities. Bring your intelligence to DIA. US citizenship is required. DIA is an equal opportunity employer.
www.dia.mil
Committed to Excellence in Defense of the Nation

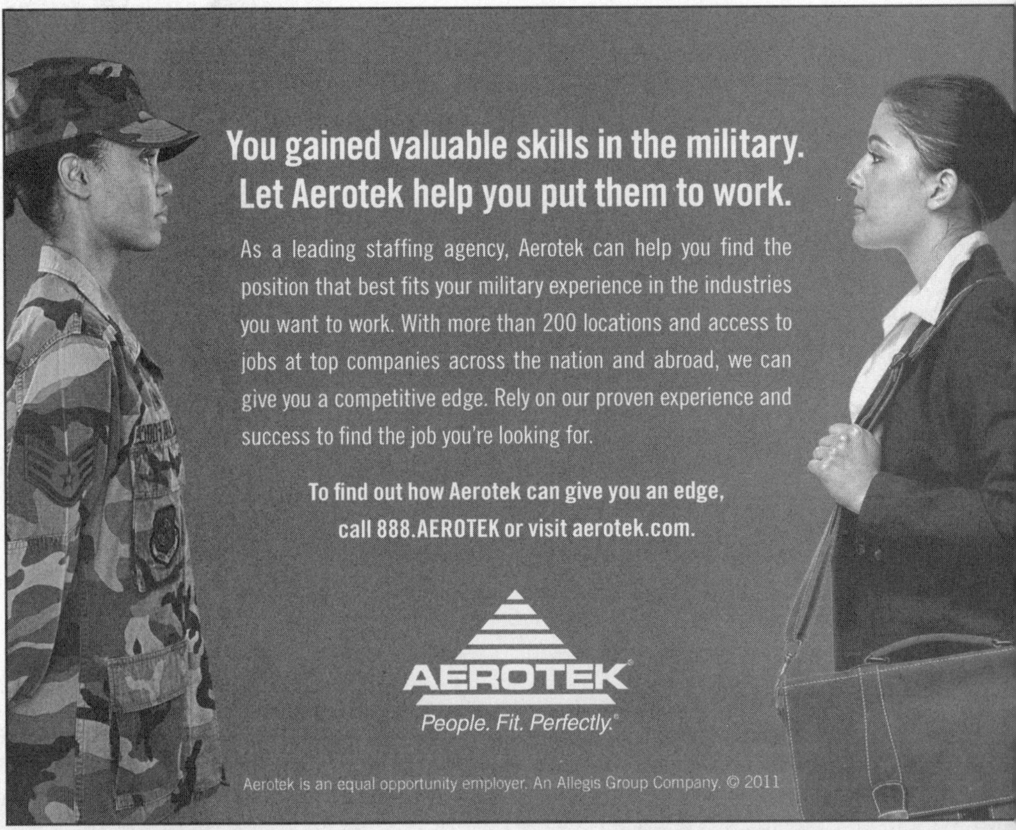

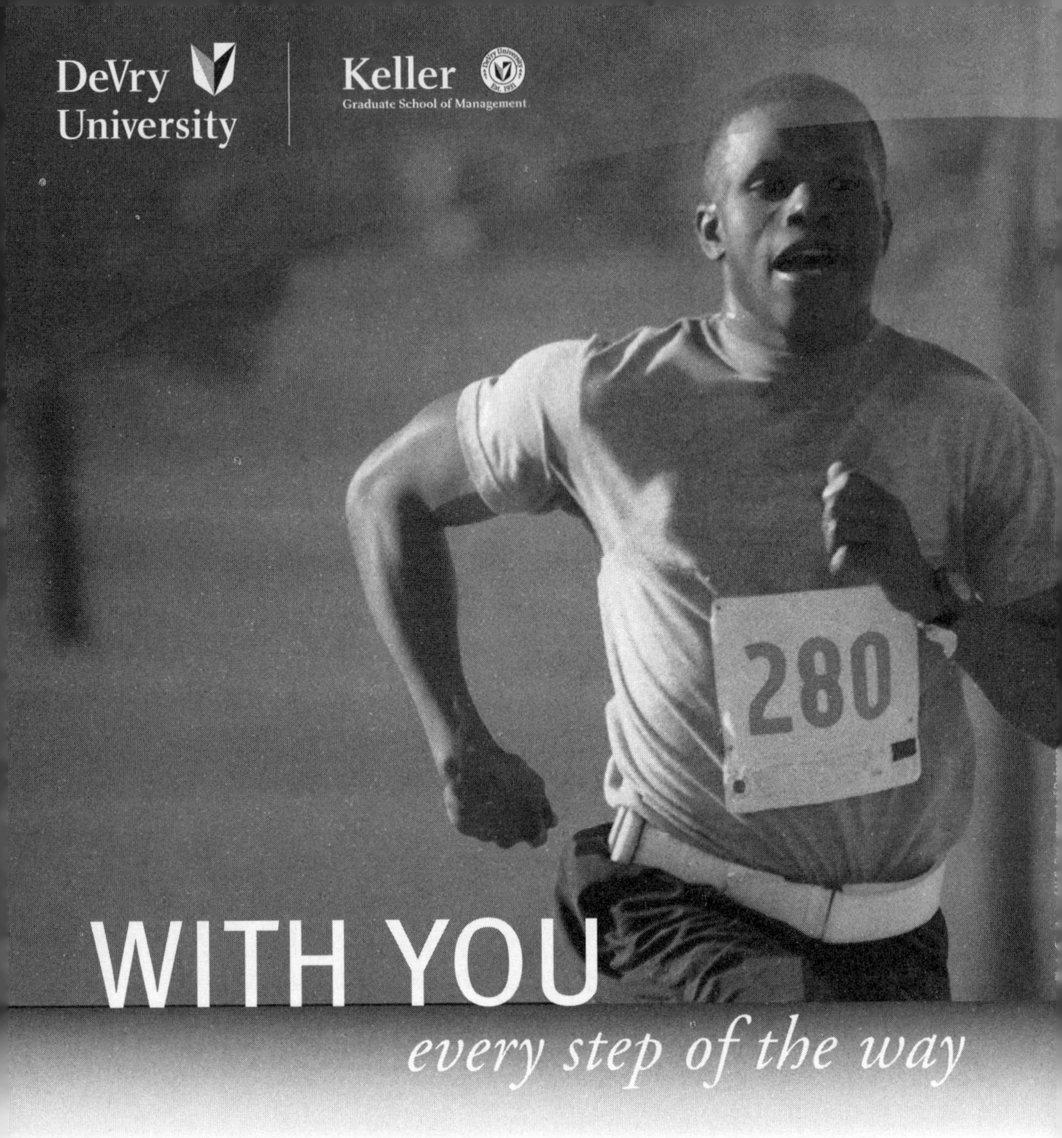

U.S. NAVY

Your **spark** makes us
Walmart
Sam's Club

ACCELERATE YOUR CAREER!

ZERO TO BACHELOR'S IN 2.5®

ONLINE & ON-CAMPUS

Virginia Beach • Norfolk, VA

Classes Starting Soon!

Call: 866.499.0336

Visit: ecpi.edu

Earn your Bachelor's Degree in 2.5 Years or your Associate's Even Sooner Through our Year-round Schedule

Network Security
Electronics Engineering Technology
Criminal Justice
Homeland Security
Business Administration
Healthcare Administration
Nursing
Culinary Arts
AND MORE...

WHY CHOOSE ECPI UNIVERSITY?

- Approved for VA/TA
- Yellow Ribbon Participating School
- Ask About Credit for Prior Military Training

Master of Science Degree in Information Systems Also Available.

School of Health Science of ECPI University

School of Culinary Arts of ECPI University

LD1061

CHENEGA CORPORATION
Work That Matters...
A Leading Alaska Native Corporation and Successful Government Contractor with Worldwide Career Opportunities in the Following Areas:
Base Operations & Maintenance
Environmental Managment
Healthcare Solutions
Information Technology & Management
Intel & Military Operations
Light Manufacturing
Linguistics Support
Logistics Support
Security Services
Telecommunications
Training Services
Transformation
Transportation
Apply online at www.chenega.com
Chenega Corporation is an EOE/AA/M/F/D/V.
Native preference under PL-93-638
Superior Benefits Package • Diverse Career Opportunities • Positive Work Environment • Competitive Salaries • Generous Incentives

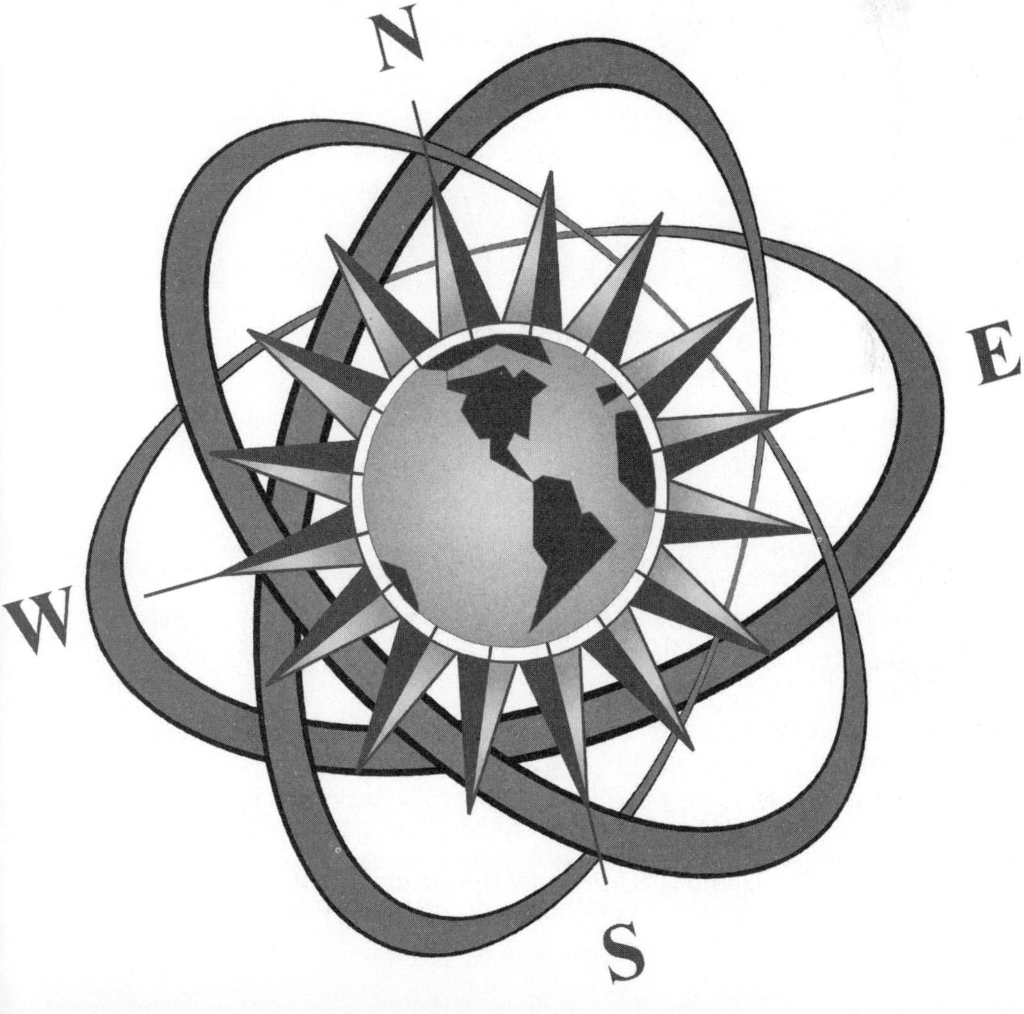

chapter 1

Welcome to the Rest of Your Life

LET'S TALK THE TRUTH about your future—you're now in charge! Thus far you've had a successful military career. But now you're making a career transition that has major life-changing implications for you and those around you. It's probably unlike any transition you have ever experienced before and unlike any you will ever experience again. With this book you should be able to plan, execute, and manage your transition to the civilian work world.

The purpose of this book is to provide you with the best assistance possible based upon our many combined years of career transition and job search experience. We want to make sure you do this right—clarify your goals, get you moving in the right direction, save you time and effort, minimize your costs, and help you connect with an excellent first post-service job that leads to a new and rewarding career. We've got lots of work to do in the hours, days, and weeks ahead. If you stay with us for the duration of this book, you should acquire several useful tips that will have a significant impact on you and your future worklife.

Question Your Future

All of life's transitions should begin with a series of basic soul-searching questions, for, in posing the right questions, you will begin to develop appropriate responses to your career transition situation.

Let's begin by examining your future and your ability to shape it with these orienting questions:

- What do you want to do with the rest of your life?
- Are you leaving the military for greener pastures?
- Are you more concerned with finding a rewarding job or pursuing a satisfying lifestyle?
- What will you most likely do well and enjoy doing in the civilian world?
- How well prepared are you for finding employment in the new job markets of today and tomorrow?

- Do you know how to write an excellent resume that translates your military experience into desirable civilian job qualifications?
- Do you know how to communicate your qualifications to employers in civilian work language?
- Are you prepared to research employers, write job-winning cover letters, network for job leads, conduct job interviews, and negotiate salary and benefits?
- Would you be better off starting your own business?
- Where do you plan to relocate and how much will it cost you?
- If you are married, how involved will your spouse be in your job search?
- Does your spouse share your transition concerns and career goals?
- Can your spouse clearly articulate your greatest strengths, evaluate your job search progress, and generally support you at every stage in your job search?
- Are you financially prepared for retirement?

We've got a big, challenging, and exciting task ahead of us. Together we will try to raise the right questions and guide you into answers appropriate to your situation. If you are like many others who have followed the advice of this book, you will discover your career transition work can be both interesting and fun. If done properly, it will make a difference in your life. In fact, it may change your life forever. Along the way, you are likely to renew some old acquaintances and meet lots of new people who will likely have a positive impact on your upcoming life change.

We're delighted to be two of the first new people you're meeting on this road to renewed career success. We're here to help—a good friend and coach if you need one. So let's get started on what should be an exciting journey into a new world of rewarding work.

Life Goes On and On and On

These and numerous other career transition questions and issues provide the central focus for this book. The reality of military jobs and careers is that they eventually come to an end for everyone involved. And in today's environment, they often come to an end faster than most people ever expected. Someday, everyone in the military must go through the career transition process. Your time happens to be now. So take a positive, proactive approach to finding the "right" job or retirement opportunity that leads to a satisfying post-military life.

Whether you are being pushed or pulled into the civilian job arena doesn't really make much difference. The fact is that you're making a career transition in which your past may provide little guidance on how to best chart your future. How you make that transition has important implications for both your personal and professional lives. Therefore, it's extremely important to focus on how you will manage this transition from the military to the civilian work world. It's the **transition process**—not different jobs or employers—that should be your central focus. You need a clear sense of where you have been, where you are at present, and where you want to go with the rest of your life. You do this by focusing on your career transition—past, present, and future.

All good things come to an end, and life does indeed go on. If you've really loved the jobs you had in your military career, chances are you will really love your next series of jobs in your civilian career as well. But you'll have to be diligent at finding your right "fit" in the civilian world. It won't happen overnight and there are no magic pills to make what may be a difficult transition quickly go away. You'll need to do some serious thinking and planning, starting with setting goals, assessing your skills, and charting a course of action aimed at finding the right job for you. You may want to involve other people in this process. If you are married, make sure your spouse is involved early on.

Chances and Choices

Chances are, you are planning to do something rewarding in your next work life. Some transitioning military personnel retire completely; they have the means and motivation to enjoy a leisurely lifestyle. But most military personnel go on to second, third, and fourth careers. Many become employees in large corporations, small businesses, and government. Others decide to start their own businesses immediately upon leaving the military or after a few years of work experience in the civilian business world. For them, the most critical transition is made upon leaving the service for their first post-military civilian job.

If done properly, this transition can lead to a most rewarding career. If done haphazardly, the transition may result in finding the wrong job, leaving within the first year, and wandering on to other inappropriate jobs. Some people become unhappy job-hoppers who communicate the wrong messages to potential employers. Unfortunately, they repeat this pattern of job disappointment and career failure for the rest of their work life. This should not happen to you.

You have excellent skills, experience, and work habits that are readily marketable in the civilian work world. But what you most need to know is how to best present and market your skills and experience in today's difficult job market. You do this by acquiring another set of skills you may or may not at present possess—job search skills. Do you know, for example, how to best write and market a job-winning resume? What networking is, and how to use it in a job search? How to locate the best employers based on your experience and skills? What the best ways are to get job information, advice, and referrals? How you can negotiate a salary 20 percent higher than expected?

You will be able to clearly answer these job search questions once you develop or refine your job search skills. The chapters that follow acquaint you with the most important job search skills for making that all-important career transition.

Welcome to a Tough Job Market

Perhaps you've never really had to look for a job. When was the last time you assessed your skills, formulated a job objective, conducted occupational research, wrote a resume and job search letters, responded to classified ads, completed online application forms, networked for information, advice, and referrals, or negotiated a salary? These are things you must learn to do effectively if you are to make a satisfying career transition.

Chances are your job search skills are either nonexistent or very rusty. If you've been out of the civilian job market for five or more years, you'll quickly discover today's job market is very different than when you left. The jobs are different, employers are different, skill requirements are more demanding, and salaries and benefits are tougher than ever to negotiate. Good jobs—those that are secure, high paying, and enjoyable—are more difficult than ever to find. Once found, good jobs are more difficult than ever to keep. You may quickly discover the job you land today may disappear within 12 to 24 months. Indeed, recent studies indicate that 40 percent of the working population goes to bed each night worried about whether they will have a job tomorrow! This should not happen to you.

One thing is certain about today's job market—it is uncertain, and highly competitive. It can be ruthless in its treatment of job seekers and employees. Frequent layoffs, firings, and downsizings testify to its insensitive and unforgiving nature. If not approached properly, the job market may result in numerous bumps and bruises for you. You may quickly discover your career success in the military lacks a clear counterpart in the civilian world.

Best Jobs For the 21st Century

The job market has changed significantly in the past decade. Today, individuals with the right education, skills, and experience are in a better position to find good jobs that should lead to career advancement in the years ahead. In fact, the U.S. Department of Labor's employment statistics to the year 2018 identify the following as the fastest growing occupations (www.bls.gov/emp/ep_table_103.htm):

Fastest Growing Occupations, 2008-2018

(Numbers in thousands of jobs)

Occupation Title	% Change	Number of New Jobs	Wages (May 2008 Median)	Education/Training Category
• Biomedical engineers	72	12	$77,400	Bachelor's degree
• Network systems & data communications analysts	53	156	71,100	Bachelor's degree
• Home health aides	50	461	20,460	Short-term on-the-job training
• Personal and home care aides	46	376	19,180	Short-term on-the-job training
• Financial examiners	41	11	70,930	Bachelor's degree
• Medical scientists, except epidemiologists	40	44	72,590	Doctoral degree
• Physician assistants	39	29	81,230	Master's degree
• Skin care specialists	38	15	28,730	Postsecondary vocational award
• Biochemists and biophysicists	37	9	82,840	Doctoral degree
• Athletic trainers	37	6	39,640	Bachelor's degree
• Physical therapist aides	36	17	23,760	Short-term on-the-job training
• Dental hygienists	36	63	66,570	Associate degree
• Veterinary technologists and technicians	36	29	28,900	Associate degree
• Dental assistants	36	106	32,380	Moderate-term on-the-job training
• Computer software engineers, applications	34	175	85,430	Bachelor's degree
• Medical assistants	34	164	28,300	Moderate-term on-the-job training
• Physical therapist assistants	33	21	46,140	Associate degree
• Veterinarians	33	20	79,050	First professional degree
• Self-enrichment education teachers	32	81	35,720	Work experience in a related occupation
• Compliance officers, except agriculture, construction, health and safety, and transportation	31	81	48,890	Long-term on-the-job training

SOURCE: BLS Occupational Employment Statistics and Division of Occupational Outlook

These employment projections confirm what we know is the major trend for the best jobs of the future—they all require greater investments in education and training. For more information on job trends, see the Bureau of Labor Statistics' *Occupational Outlook Handbook* at www.bls.gov/oco.

The New Flat and Entrepreneurial World

Underlying these job projections are important changes in the global economy that may have an adverse impact on your employment future. India and China, with a combined population of 2.3 billion and rapidly developing, well educated, skilled, and consumer-oriented middle classes, are transforming the U.S. business and employment scenes. The job you have today may well go to these countries because of the convergence of seven important developments:

1. improved Internet connections and increased bandwidth
2. powerful fiber optic cable
3. cheap international telecom prices
4. large pool of well-trained English-speaking workers in developing countries
5. efficient international transportation links and delivery services
6. enhanced global organization and management systems
7. new supply-chain systems strategically centered around mega airport-based cities (aerotroplis)

As Thomas L. Friedman persuasively argues in *The World Is Flat: A Brief History of the Twenty-First Century* (Farrar, Straus, and Giroux, 2005), in the rapidly changing global economy there are no American jobs—only jobs that go to the lowest bidder. By implication, Friedman's new flat (interconnected and complex) world will generate few well-paying jobs. An increasing number of jobs—both low- and high-tech—go to the cheapest and most efficient workers in the world, who are increasingly found in India, China, Vietnam, Cambodia, the Philippines, Indonesia, South Africa, Mexico, Costa Rica, and a host of other Third and Fourth World countries rather than in high-cost Los Angeles, Seattle, Chicago, Detroit, Cincinnati, Washington, DC, Atlanta, or Miami.

If you want a competitive edge in this new global economy, the most important skill you need to acquire is the **ability to learn**. The best jobs disproportionately favor smart workers who are quick on their feet because they are constantly learning new skills, adapting to changing markets, and producing goods and services both inexpensively and efficiently. In such a world, employers are constantly under pressure to cut production and service costs, which means keeping labor costs low by reducing benefits, controlling salary and wage increases, and cutting legacy (primarily pension) costs. Successful entrepreneurs, especially small business owners, understand how to quickly adapt to and best navigate this global economy to their advantage. Individuals rather than large bureaucratic organizations have a distinct advantage in navigating this fast-changing global economy. In the flat world, the entrepreneur is king.

Getting Started Right

Where do you start, and what should you do first? The process of making a career transition is not really difficult. Almost anyone can find a job. But finding a good job is hard work. Much of what is involved in finding a job is common sense and follows a rational decision-making model as outlined in Chapter 2. In the military, you are used to setting goals, developing plans, and focusing on accomplishing the mission. Therefore, the job-finding process should make good sense to you. You'll initially recognize the process as nothing more than good planning and implementation meeting common sense. You'll later discover the job search is much more than this, too.

At the same time, you are dealing with a chaotic job market in which information on job vacancies and employers is difficult to access, the rules for finding jobs are inconsistent, and the screening process seems unpredictable and unfair. Rational planning applied to a chaotic environment beyond your control can lead to numerous rejections, disappointments, and frustrations. As you attempt to accomplish a mission in such an uncertain environment, you will discover the wonderful world of **serendipity**—chance occurrences that may unexpectedly lead to the right job for you. Always keep your mind and eyes open for serendipity. It's what makes chaos tolerable, forgiving, and unexpectedly rewarding.

Our job-finding process in Chapter 2 follows 10 well-defined career planning and job search steps involving investigation, written communication, and employer contact activities. Successful job seekers learn to plan and implement each of these sequential steps. Each step involves important planning, organizational, and communication skills. They require constant practice through daily, routinized job search activities.

Don't Forget Your Concerned Spouse

Funny things happen on the way to a new job and career. Unemployed people will tell you that looking for a job is no fun. It's difficult on both the ego and the family. Rejections are terrible experiences, especially if you have been used to receiving respect based on your military rank and position and if you have been feeling successful in what you do. Change your job and you'll quickly discover how different life can be. Your support system changes. Rank and position not tied to demonstrated performance don't count for much in the civilian work world. You'll have to quickly establish credibility with strangers, who know little or nothing about your background, talents, and capabilities to perform in their organization.

If you are married, don't forget your spouse on the way to finding the right job. Time and again we've discovered many transitioning military personnel are unrealistic about their future careers. Many have inflated expectations about their value to civilian employers. Because of their success in the military, they believe the job search process will be relatively easy—just develop a sound plan and implement it. But their spouses know better. They understand that this transition will probably not be easy and the end result could be less than satisfactory if not done properly. Sometimes these feelings result in a spouse pressuring their husband or wife to find a job quickly. The results can be disastrous—a bad job fit, an unhappy work situation, frequent job-hopping, and increased family tensions. Nothing fits right!

To avoid this problem, we recommend involving your spouse early in the career transition process. Use each other as a sounding board for exploring career alternatives, examining new ideas, assessing your progress, and keeping your job search focused and realistic. Better still, you may want to conduct two job searches together!

The process of finding a job can be an extremely ego-deflating process. Therefore, it's important that you find **supports** along the way. As you will see in Chapter 3, each branch of service within the Department of Defense offers a wide range of services to assist you with your career transition. These support services come in the form of job search assistance, career counseling, resume writing, and much, much more. The people who provide these services have one goal in mind—to assist you in making a successful transition. Make sure you take advantage of these excellent support services!

As in most ventures in life, he who perseveres succeeds. So stay positive, involve your spouse early in the job search process, and enjoy the journey.

Planning and the Art of Sailing Into Your Future

We wish you well as you embark on what should become an exciting yet challenging process of finding a job and career right for you. The chapters that follow are designed to guide you through the key steps in the career transition process. We include the latest job search strategies and techniques that work for thousands of job seekers. They will work for you if you organize yourself properly and take the time to put them into practice.

To be most successful, you will need to be purposeful, patient, persistent, enthusiastic, and a bit irrational in your approach to the transition process. Approach your career transition as an exciting adventure that will result in a rewarding lifestyle for you and your family.

Please don't confuse job search planning with strategic military planning—a mistake often made by inexperienced job seekers. Such an analogy is inappropriate given the relatively unstructured nature of the civilian job market and the general lack of centralized decision-making points, coherent communication channels, and visible power centers. Planning and organization in a job search does not mean creating a detailed plan, greenprint, or road map for taking action. Implementation according to a detailed plan simply doesn't work when dealing with the civilian job market.

The role of planning in your job search should approximate the art of sailing: you know where you want to go and the general direction for getting there. But the specific path, as well as the time for reaching your destination, will be determined by your environment, situation, and skills. Like the sailor dependent upon his or her sailing skills and environmental conditions, you tack back and forth, progressing within what is an acceptable time period for successful completion of the task.

Your plan should not become an **end**—it should be a flexible **means** for achieving your stated job and career goals. Planning makes sense, because it requires you to set goals and develop strategies for achieving the goals. Too much planning can blind you to unexpected occurrences and opportunities.

In the end, you'll discover sailing is really what your job search is all about. If you stay with us long enough, you're going to learn to sail very well, perhaps beyond your wildest expectations. You'll learn a great deal about yourself and others in the job market. Best of all, you're going to turn what may initially appear to be a problem into one of the most exciting times of your life.

We wish you smooth sailing as you chart your course for a new and exciting career and/or lifestyle that will help make a positive transition for the rest of your life.

For more assistance in developing your career transition plan, visit www.CorporateGray.com and click the Transition Guide tab.

chapter 2

Get Organized for New Successes

YOU ARE JOINING MILLIONS of other individuals who go through job and career transitions each year. Indeed, between 15 and 20 million people find themselves unemployed each year. Millions of others try to increase their satisfaction within the workplace as well as advance their careers by looking for alternative jobs and careers.

If you are like most other Americans, you will make more than 10 job changes and three to five career changes during your lifetime. The fact that you have spent many years in the military where you have already made several job changes probably means you will make at least two more career changes and six job changes during the rest of your work-life. You are now engaging in the first of what may become several such changes in your future.

Planning Your Successful Transition

Most people make job or career transitions by accident. While luck does play a role in finding employment, we recommend that you **plan** for future job and career changes. As a member of the military, you can begin planning your luck by using several free or low-cost transition services designed for military personnel. We'll examine these in Chapter 3.

Finding a job or changing a career in a systematic and well-planned manner is hard yet rewarding work. The task should first be based upon a clear understanding of the key ingredients that define jobs and careers. Starting with this understanding, you should next convert key concepts into action steps for implementing your job search.

A career is a series of related jobs which have common skill, interest, and motivational bases. You may change jobs several times without changing careers. But once you change skills, interests, and motivations, you change careers.

It's not easy to find a job given the present structure of the job market as well as the disappearance of jobs. You will find the job market to be relatively disorganized, although it projects an outward appearance of coherence. If you seek comprehensive, accurate, and timely job information, the job market will frustrate you with its poor communication. While you will find employment services ready to assist you, such services tend to be fragmented and their performance is often disappointing. Numerous job search methods also may be ineffective.

No system is organized to give people jobs. At best you will encounter a decentralized and fragmented system consisting of job listings in newspapers, trade journals, employment offices, or computerized job databases—all designed to link potential candidates with available job openings. Many people will try to sell you job information as well as questionable job search services. While efforts have been made to create a nationwide job bank which would list available job vacancies on a daily basis, such efforts have been unsuccessful. Instead, the government and several commercial firms have created numerous competing online, searchable databases for both job seekers and employers. In the end, most systems organized to help you find a job do not provide you with the information you need in order to land a job that is most related to your skills and interests.

Understand and Organize Your Job Search

Finding a job is both an art and a science; it encompasses a variety of basic facts, principles, and skills which can be learned but which also must be adapted to individual situations. Thus, learning how to find a job can be as important to career success as knowing how to perform a job. Indeed, job-finding skills are often more important to career success than job performance or work-content skills.

The diagram on the next page examines the key elements in a successful job search. It consists of a 10-step process which relates your past, present, and future. We will cover steps 4-10 in subsequent chapters which deal with skills assessment, research, resume writing, networking, interviewing, and salary negotiations.

Based on this concept, your past is well integrated into the process of finding a job or changing your career. Therefore, you should feel comfortable conducting your job search: it represents the best of what you are in terms of your past and present accomplishments as these relate to your present and future goals. If you base your job search on this process concept, you will communicate your best self to employers as well as focus on your strengths both during the job search and on the job.

Since the individual job search steps are interrelated, they should be followed in sequence. If you fail to properly complete the initial self-assessment steps, your job search may become haphazard, aimless, and costly. For example, you should never write a resume (Step 7) before first conducting an assessment of your skills (Step 4) and identifying your objective (Step 5). Relating Step 4 to Step 5 is especially critical to the successful implementation of all other job search steps. You must complete Steps 4 and 5 before continuing on to the other steps. Steps 7 to 10 may be conducted simultaneously because they complement and reinforce one another.

> Learning how to find a job is as important as knowing how to perform a job.

Try to sequence your job search as close to these steps as possible. The true value of this sequencing will become very apparent as you implement your plan.

The steps identified on the next page represent key processes used successfully by thousands of military and nonmilitary job seekers during the past 40 years. They should work for you as long as you recognize the importance of linking work-content skills with job search skills.

You must do much more than just know how to find a job. In the job markets of today and tomorrow, you need to constantly review your work-content skills to make sure they are appropriate for the changing job market. Assuming you have the necessary work-content skills for the civilian job market, you should be ready to target your skills on particular jobs and careers that you do well and enjoy doing. You will be able to avoid the trap of trying to fit into jobs that are not conducive to your particular mix of interests, abilities, skills, and motivations.

10 Steps to Job Search Success

Test Your Job Search Competencies

Knowing where the jobs are is important to your job search. But knowing how to find a job is even more important. Before you acquire names, addresses, and phone numbers of potential employers, you should possess the necessary job search knowledge and skills for gathering and using job information effectively.

Answers to many of your job-related questions are found by examining your present level of job search knowledge and skills. Successful job seekers, for example, use a great deal of information as well as specific skills and strategies for getting the jobs they want.

Let's begin by testing for the level of job search information, skills, and strategies you currently possess as well as those you need to develop and improve. You can easily identify your level of job search competence by completing the exercise on the next page.

You can calculate your overall job search competencies by adding the numbers you circled for a composite score. If your total is more than 75 points, you need to work on developing your careering skills. How you scored each item will indicate to what degree you need to work on improving specific job search skills. If your score is under 50 points, you are well on your way toward job search success. In either case, this book should help you better focus your job search as well as identify job search skills you need to acquire or strengthen.

Seek Professional Assistance When Necessary

While some people can successfully conduct a job search based on the advice of books such as this, many others also need the assistance of career professionals who offer everything from testing and assessment services to offering employer contacts, including job vacancy information and temporary employment services. Some do one-on-one career counseling while others sponsor one- to three-day workshops or six- to 12-week courses on the various steps in the career planning process. We strongly recommend you contact your nearest transition assistance office first (see Chapter 3), before investing your time and money in other career planning and job search services. The many highly qualified professional counselors you will encounter have a wealth of experience and are motivated to assist you in making a smooth transition from the military to the civilian workplace.

Options

You have two options in organizing your job search. First, you can follow the principles and advice outlined in this and many other self-directed books. Just read the chapters and then put them into practice by following the step-by-step instructions. Second, you may wish to seek professional help to either supplement or replace this book.

We recognize the value of professional assistance, especially in today's environment. With the critical assessment and objective-setting steps (Chapters 4-6), some individuals may need more assistance than our advice and exercises provide. You may, for example, want to take a battery of tests to better understand your interests and values in relation to alternative jobs and careers. And still others, due to a combination of job loss, failed relationships, or depression, may need therapy best provided by a trained psychologist or psychiatrist rather than career testing and information services provided by career counselors. If any of these situations pertain to you, by all means seek professional help.

You also should beware of pitfalls with some so-called professional career services. While many services are excellent, others are useless and some are fraudulent. We recommend always asking for the names and phone numbers of some former military personnel who have used their service and make sure you call them to gauge their level of satisfaction with the services rendered.

Your Careering Competencies

INSTRUCTIONS: Respond to each statement by circling which number at the right best represents your situation.

SCALE:
1 = strongly agree
2 = agree
3 = maybe, not certain
4 = disagree
5 = strongly disagree

1.	I know what motivates me to excel at work.	1 2 3 4 5
2.	I can identify my strongest abilities and skills.	1 2 3 4 5
3.	I have seven major achievements that clarify a pattern of interests and abilities that are relevant to my job and career.	1 2 3 4 5
4.	I know what I both like and dislike in work.	1 2 3 4 5
5.	I know what I want to do during the next 10 years.	1 2 3 4 5
6.	I have a well defined career objective that focuses my job search on particular organizations and employers.	1 2 3 4 5
7.	I know what skills I can offer employers in different occupations.	1 2 3 4 5
8.	I know what skills employers most seek in candidates.	1 2 3 4 5
9.	I can clearly explain to employers what I do well and enjoy doing.	1 2 3 4 5
10.	I can specify why employers should hire me.	1 2 3 4 5
11.	I can gain the support of family and friends for making a job or career change.	1 2 3 4 5
12.	I can find 10 to 20 hours a week to conduct a part-time job search.	1 2 3 4 5
13.	I have the financial ability to sustain a three-month job search.	1 2 3 4 5

14. I can conduct library and Internet research on different occupations, employers, organizations, and communities.	1 2 3 4 5
15. I can write different types of effective resumes and job search/thank you letters.	1 2 3 4 5
16. I can produce and distribute resumes and job search/thank you letters.	1 2 3 4 5
17. I have a clear pattern of accomplishments which I can explain to employers, citing examples.	1 2 3 4 5
18. I can identify and target employers I want to interview.	1 2 3 4 5
19. I can develop a job referral network.	1 2 3 4 5
20. I can persuade others to join in forming a job search support group.	1 2 3 4 5
21. I know which websites are best for posting my resume and browsing job postings.	1 2 3 4 5
22. I can use the telephone to develop prospects and get referrals and interviews.	1 2 3 4 5
23. I know how much time I should spend conducting an online job search.	1 2 3 4 5
24. I can generate one job interview for every 10 job search contacts I make.	1 2 3 4 5
25. I have a list of at least 10 employer-centered questions I need to ask during interviews.	1 2 3 4 5
26. I can follow up on job interviews.	1 2 3 4 5
27. I can negotiate a salary 10-15% above what an employer initially offers.	1 2 3 4 5
28. I can persuade an employer to renegotiate my salary after six months on the job.	1 2 3 4 5
29. I can create a position for myself in an organization.	1 2 3 4 5
TOTAL	________

Alternative Services

There are at least seven types of professional services through which you can receive help in career planning, job search, and employment assistance:

1. **Government-sponsored services:** The Departments of Defense, Labor, and Veterans Affairs all offer customized transition services available for free or at a very low cost to transitioning servicemembers. Within the Department of Defense, you can access the many outstanding transition services provided through your Transition Assistance Office. The Department of Veterans Affairs (VA) is your window to a wide variety of benefits and services available to you, the soon-to-be military veteran. Important to note, VA can provide you with the names and phone numbers of veteran contacts in the state employment offices. The Department of Labor's principal transition service is embodied in its Transition Assistance Program. A more detailed explanation of these programs is contained in Chapter 4.

2. **Professional associations:** Professional associations often provide placement assistance. Members of the Military Officers Association of America (MOAA) and the Non Commissioned Officers Association (NCOA) can participate in excellent career transition services specifically for their members. If you are not a member, you are well-advised to join the appropriate association before you leave the service. The primary purpose of these associations is to protect and foster the interests of military personnel—both active and retired. Detailed information on each of these is provided in Chapter 4. You should also check with other professional associations, especially those in your desired field of employment. You will find that there is a professional association for almost every civilian occupation. Some of these associations will have job search and placement services available to their members. These services usually consist of listing job vacancies and job information exchanges at annual conferences. These meetings are excellent sources for making job contacts. To find information on associations, do a Google search on "professional associations."

3. **Job fairs:** Many transitioning military have landed jobs through participation in a job fair. This is an excellent way to meet with employers who are interested in hiring people with military skills and experience. The Corporate Gray Job Fairs (www.CorporateGray.com) are held in Norfolk/Virginia Beach and Springfield, Virginia. These job fairs are free and open to job seekers of all ranks (officers and enlisted) and branches of service. Military spouses and other adult family members are welcome to attend. For a schedule of upcoming events, visit www.CorporateGray.com. NCOA also holds job fairs at various locations across the U.S. For more information, visit www.ncoausa.org. MOAA also provides a variety of career transition services for its members. For details, visit www.moaa.org/tops. Remember, whenever you attend a job fair, make sure that you are "dressed for success" and bring many copies of your resume. You can expect on-the-spot interviews with company representatives, most of whom have immediate job opportunities. Make the most of these face-to-face opportunities!

4. **Military placement agencies:** There are many military-specific placement agencies in existence. They are in the business of finding transitioning military personnel who fit the profiles of their corporate clients. Most placement agencies do not charge the job seeker a fee for their services. Instead, they are paid by their corporate clients whenever their candidates are hired by them. Consequently, military placement agencies generally only work with those candidates whose skills and experience fit with the needs of their corporate clients. Outplacement agencies, on the other hand, will generally work

with any candidate who desires to use their services (for a fee). These agencies work to prepare the candidate for a successful job search by providing personalized, individual attention. If you elect to use one of these agencies, how do you know which one is best for you? Our recommendation is to ask your friends and associates which ones have worked best for them. You should also ask the firm if they specialize in a given area or cover multiple career fields.

5. **Temporary employment firms:** During the past decade temporary employment firms have come of age as more and more employers turn to them for recruitment assistance. They offer a variety of employment services to both employers and job seekers. Many of these firms recruit individuals for a wide range of positions and skill levels as well as full-time employment. Most now offer excellent "temp-to-perm" programs which are ideally suited for transitioning military personnel wishing to upgrade their skills and acquire civilian work experience in lieu of accepting a full-time position. Indeed, if you are interested in "testing the job waters," we strongly recommend that you contact these firms for information on their services. Employers—not job seekers—pay for these services. This is a particularly good alternative for those who want to do something far afield than what you did in the military and want to see if you will truly like it.

6. **Testing and assessment centers:** Testing and assessment centers provide assistance for identifying vocational skills and interests. The most cost-effective of these can generally be found through your local community college. You may wish to use some of these services – in addition to our exercises in Chapters 4-6—to formulate your job search objective. You can find online assessments at the following websites: www. assessment.com, www.self-directed-search.com, and www.personalityonline.com.

7. **Professional resume writers and career coaches:** Several reputable professionals assist job seekers in organizing and implementing an effective job search. Contact these organizations to find a certified professional for assistance:

   - **National Board for Certified Counselors, Inc.** www.nbcc.org
   - **National Career Development Association** www.ncda.org
   - **Certified Career Coaches** www.certifiedcareercoaches.com
   - **Professional Association of Resume Writers & Career Coaches** www.parw.com

When in Doubt, Take Action

The old adage "When in doubt, do something" is especially relevant when expanded to include a thoughtful plan of action related to the job search process: "When in doubt, engage in a concrete activity related to the sequence of job search steps." This might include conducting research on communities, companies, positions, and salaries; surveying job vacancy announcements; writing a resume and job search letters; or contacting three employers each day.

But developing a plan and taking action is much easier said than done. If conducted properly, a job search can become an extremely time-consuming activity. It inevitably competes with other personal and professional priorities. That's why you need to make some initial decisions as to how and when you will conduct a job search. How much time are you willing to set aside each day or week to engage in each of the seven job search activities outlined at the beginning of this chapter? After you've spent numerous hours identifying your abilities and skills and formulating an objective, are you willing to commit yourself to 20 hours a week to network for information and advice? If you are unwilling to commit both your time and yourself to each activity within the process, you may remain stuck, and inevitably frustrated, at the initial stages of self-awareness and understanding. Success only comes to those who take action at all stages in the job search process.

Use Your Time Wisely

If you decide to conduct your own job search with minimum assistance from professionals, your major cost will be your time. Therefore, you must find sufficient time to devote to your job search. Ask yourself this question: "How valuable is my time in relation to finding a job or changing my career?" Assign a dollar value to your time. For example, is your time worth $3, $5, $10, $25, $50, or $100 an hour? Compare your figure with what you might pay a professional for doing much of the job search work for you. Normal professional fees range from $2,000 to $12,000.

The amount of time you can devote to your job search will depend on your personal situation. We understand that until you actually separate or retire from the military, you are employed by the U.S. government and have a job to do. However, we also realize that you probably don't work 24 hours per day. Therefore, as time allows, we recommend you concentrate on your job search sooner rather than later and make maximum use of the time available. There are certain advantages that accrue to seeking a new job while still employed. Because you are employed and have key benefits like health coverage, you usually appear more attractive to prospective employers, who may view unemployed candidates as more likely to take the first job available. Remember, your goal is to find a job based on your strengths rather than your needs.

A simple yet effective technique for improving your time management practices is to complete a "to do" list for each day. This list also should prioritize which activities are most important to accomplish each day. Include at the top of your list a particular job search activity or several activities that should be completed that day. If you follow this simple time management practice, you will find the necessary time to include your job search in your daily routine. You can give your job search top priority. Better still, you will accomplish more in less time, and with better results.

Plan to Take Action . . . and Get Lucky

While we recommend that you plan your job search, we also caution you to avoid the excesses of too much planning. Like time management, planning should not be all-consuming. Planning makes sense because it focuses attention and directs action toward specific goals and targets. It requires you to set goals and develop strategies for achieving the goals. However, too much planning can blind you to unexpected opportunities—that wonderful experience called serendipity. Luck—being in the right place at the right time—plays an important role in the job search. However, we like to plan our luck. After all, luck is when preparation and opportunity meet.

Given the highly decentralized and chaotic nature of the job market, you want to do just enough planning so you will be in a position to take advantage of what will inevitably be unexpected occurrences and opportunities arising from your planned job search activities. Therefore, as you plan your job search, be sure you are flexible enough to take advantage of new opportunities and the luck that inevitably will come your way.

Develop an Action-Oriented Timeline

As with any military operation, it is important to establish a timeline and be disciplined in the execution of your planned activities. It is no less important when embarking on your employment campaign. Your mission is to obtain employment. Therefore, you need to consider doing the following:

1. Determine the number of weeks/months before you need to start the new job. It's never too early to start!
2. Prioritize the employment search activities.
3. Determine which activities can be done concurrently or must be done sequentially.
4. Place activities on a timeline.
5. Execute the plan.
6. Follow up each job search activity with appropriate actions.

Developing a sound yet flexible search plan is critical to conducting a successful employment campaign. Regardless of how much time you have, the time spent planning and organizing your activities will result in a far more effective job search.

A timeline is one technique you should include in your job search for planning your activities. Here's an example of what you may want to sequence on your timeline:

FIRST MONTH:

- Determine your employment desires (read job search books with major sections on self-assessment and goal setting).
- Contact your local Transition Assistance Program office to obtain a schedule of transition classes.
- Contact your college's alumni office or that of a local community college to identify available career transition services.
- Make a list of your friends and colleagues whom you believe would be willing to talk about the corporate world.
- Look at your wardrobe—think about what clothes you will need to buy. Begin watching the newspaper or TV for sales.

SECOND MONTH:

- Attend transition classes
- **Prepare your resume (see Chapter 7):**
  - Read career transition and job search books and articles
  - Draft a resume for the positions you are seeking. (You will probably want to use a "combination resume" which highlights your functional skills and also tells the prospective employer the nature of your assignments.)
  - Consult with professional career counselors (see Chapter 3) for assistance in helping you translate your military experience into civilian terms.
  - Post your resume to TurboTAP (www.turbotap.org) and other employment sites, such as Corporate Gray Online (www.CorporateGray.com)
- **Research employment fields:**
  - Visit the library and explore the Internet—learn about the different companies that exist in your fields of interest.
  - See our research and networking advice in Chapter 9 and 10.
- **Start informational interviews (see Chapter 11):**
  - Contact your friends and associates on the list you made last month and make an appointment to meet with them.
  - Prepare for the interviews—think about questions you will ask; research different fields, companies, and industries.
  - At the interview—ask intelligent questions; listen; thank them for their time.
- Join an association in your field of interest. Attend the next meeting.

THIRD MONTH:

- Contact some placement agencies—let them know about your qualifications, career interests, etc. Ask for suggestions.
- Continue informational interviewing.
- Join another association in your desired career field. Network with members.
- Update your records—track whom you've met, what transpired, future actions.
- Expand your wardrobe—purchase a second interview suit.
- Identify potential references—contact them; send copies of your resume.
- Write to those firms that are involved in the type of work in which you are interested.
- Respond to selected newspaper ads for employment (after researching the firm at the library or on the Web).
- Attend local job fairs and career conferences.
- Continue to expand your network contacts through informational interviews.

FOURTH AND SUBSEQUENT MONTHS:

- Follow up on all employment leads.
- Stay in touch with your contacts, references, and executive recruiters.

Depending on your situation, you may want to develop a timeline which incorporates a different sequence of job search activities. However, your overall job search should follow the job search steps we previously discussed.

Your timeline should incorporate the individual job search activities over a six-month period. If you phase in the first five job search steps during the initial three to four weeks and continue the final four steps in subsequent weeks and months, you should begin receiving job offers within two to three months after initiating your job search. Interviews and job offers can come anytime—often unexpectedly—as you conduct your job search. An average time is three months, but it can occur within a week or take as long as five months. If you plan, prepare, and persist, the pay-off will be job interviews and offers.

While three to six months may seem a long time—especially if you are unemployed—you can shorten your job search time by increasing the frequency of your individual job search activities. If you are job hunting on a full-time basis, you may be able to cut your job search time in half. But don't expect to get a job that's right for you within a week or two. Job hunting requires time and hard work—perhaps the hardest work you will ever do—but if done properly, it pays off with a job that is right for you.

Strategies for Success

Success is determined by more than just a good plan or timeline getting implemented. We know success is not determined primarily by intelligence, time management, or luck. Based upon experience, theory, research, common sense, and some self-transformation principles, we believe you will achieve job search success by following many of these 20 principles:

1. Work hard at finding a job
2. Do not be discouraged by setbacks
3. Be patient and persevere
4. Be honest with yourself and others
5. Develop a positive attitude toward yourself
6. Associate with positive and successful people
7. Set goals and plan
8. Get organized
9. Be a good communicator

10. Be energetic and enthusiastic
11. Ask questions
12. Be a good listener
13. Be polite, courteous, and thoughtful
14. Be tactful
15. Maintain a professional stance
16. Demonstrate your intelligence and competence
17. Maximize your contacts through networking
18. Do not over-do your job search
19. Be open-minded and keep on the lookout for "luck"
20. Evaluate your progress and make adjustments

These principles should provide you with an initial orientation for starting your job search. As you become more experienced, you will develop your own set of operating principles that should work for you in particular employment situations.

Take Risks and Handle Rejections

Job hunting is a highly ego-involved activity which will probably result in numerous **rejections** you may take personally. After all, you place your past, abilities, and self-image before strangers who don't know who you are or what you can do. Being rejected, or having someone say "no" to you, will probably be your greatest job hunting difficulty. We know most people can handle two or three "no's" before they get discouraged. If you approach your job search from a less ego-involved perspective, you can take "no's. The more rejections you get, the more acceptances you receive. Therefore, you must normally encounter rejection before you get acceptances.

Organize Your Job Search

On a practical level, there are certain tools that we suggest using to organize your job search. First, you will want to use a calendar to keep track of your various job search related appointments. Second, establish a task list to help you identify and manage the various tasks that are part of your job search. Third, use a contact manager tool, like GoldMine or Act!, to help you manage contact information and to track the outcome of your discussions. Fourth, use a filing system with folders and sub-folders to help you find job search items quickly. The more organized you become, the more efficient your job search.

Join or Form a Support Group

We believe most people can conduct a successful job search on their own by following the step-by-step procedures outlined in this book. Our self-directed methods work well when you join others in forming a job search group. The group provides a certain degree of security which is often necessary when launching a new and unknown venture. In addition, the group can provide important information on job leads. Members will critique your approach and progress. They will provide you with psychological supports as you experience the frustration of rejections and the joys of success. You also will be helping others who will be helping you.

To track your progress, download a planning worksheet by visiting www.CorporateGray.com. *While there, also download and take the Career Competency Assessment.*

chapter 3

Obtain Transition Assistance

YOU DON'T HAVE TO FACE your career transition alone. As noted in this Chapter, you will find numerous organizations and individuals eager to assist you with career transition and job search services. Many of these services are free or require a nominal fee, while others can be very expensive. The quality of these services varies widely, from outstanding to poor. For the uninitiated, selecting the right services and choosing the best quality organizations and individuals to assist you can present truly bewildering choices. Let's try to sort through this maze.

You need to make the right choices for transition assistance. We recommend starting out "close to home" for such assistance. The Department of Defense, the military services, various federal and state agencies, and even military-related associations sponsor high quality transition services you should use throughout your job search. We strongly recommend taking advantage of the lectures, seminars, and testing services offered by these agencies.

We cannot overemphasize the importance of using these free or low-cost services early in the job transition process. The transition professionals staffing these services are highly skilled in their respective fields and will help steer you in the right direction. In this chapter we describe these services and reveal how to obtain additional information.

Forms and Employment Restrictions

One of the first actions you should take after making the separation/retirement decision is to visit the office of your base's Staff Judge Advocate General or servicing legal office. It's important to know the legal restrictions placed on servicemembers who separate or retire from active duty. This is especially true for retiring regular officers who have served in the acquisition or procurement fields. Therefore, you need to:

1. **Know the post-retirement or separation rules:**
    - Pre-employment restrictions (18 U.S.C. 208)
    - Post-employment restrictions (18 U.S.C. 207, 10 U.S.C. 2397, 41 U.S.C. 423)
2. **Report job contacts:**
    - Disqualification statements/recusals (18 U.S.C. 208, 10 U.S.C. 2397A)

3. **Obtain required forms prior to separation:**
    - DD Form 1787: Report of DoD and Defense Related Employment. Majors and above must file within 90 days of employment with any major defense contractor.

Your base legal office can provide more detailed information on required forms and on employment prohibitions and restrictions affecting your situation.

Military Transition Services

Air Force Transition Assistance Program

The Air Force offers the Transition Assistance Program (TAP) at every active duty Air Force base through the Airman and Family Readiness Centers. The Transition Assistance Program provides direct assistance and counseling to transitioning servicemembers and their families in order to provide them with the tools they need for a successful transition to civilian life. (Note: Although the names are similar, this TAP is an Air Force program, and is not the same as the TAP Workshops co-sponsored by the Departments of Labor and Veterans Affairs, which are described elsewhere in this chapter.) The Air Force program is mandated by Congress, augmented by Air Force family support policies, and administered by the Airman and Family Readiness Centers. Each center has a TAP staff which serves all separating and retiring members. Servicemembers within 180 days of separation or retirement receive priority consideration.

Through the Transition Assistance Program, you can find a variety of transition programs, as outlined below. In addition, personnel and families from any military branch can utilize the Airman and Family Readiness Center at any installation so Air Force personnel can also take advantage of the programs provided by the other service branches.

Just as networking expands your possible range of job contacts, taking advantage of all of the TAP services expands your horizons as well. By participating in the many programs offered through TAP, you can make the most of your career change. The TAP includes:

Counseling:

- Benefits, Entitlements, and Services
- Individual Transition Plan
- DD Forms 2586, Verification of Military Experience and Training (VMET)
- Resume preparation/critique
- Department of Labor TAP Workshops

Job Search Assistance:

- Workshops on Job Search Strategies, Resume Writing, Interview Techniques, Owning Your Own Business, Federal Careers, Career Planning, Job Survival Skills, Job Hunting Skills, Career Dressing Techniques, and more.
- Resource centers containing labor market information, wage and salary guides, and statistical surveys (e.g., Department of Commerce economic forecasts)
- Testing and assessment programs to determine interest and skills inventories (e.g., Myers-Briggs, Discover, Strong Interest Inventory)
- Access to computers, faxes, and copying equipment
- Automated resume design/writing programs and federal employment software
- Employer information databases
- Computerized job bank listing featuring state, federal, and local area jobs
- Job Clubs: information and networking groups

Family Transition Skills:

- Career Focus Program for Spouse Employment
- Stress Management

The Family Support Center provides other programs to help transitioning members and their families adjust to a new civilian lifestyle, including:

- Relocation Assistance Program
- Personal Financial Management Program
- Family Life Education
- Information and Referral Program

The Air Force education, housing, military personnel, transportation management, and chaplain's offices assist separatees with guidance, counseling, and information on career awareness, college and vocational training, moving and storage, and separation benefits.

The Departments of Labor and Veterans Affairs provide TAP Workshops and counsel transitioning airmen on veterans' benefits at Air Force installations throughout the continental U.S. Department of Labor approved TAP Workshops are presented at all overseas bases by TAP transition staff members.

The transition programs at each base are tailored to meet the needs of the servicemembers in that community. For that reason, there may be minor differences among the programs offered at these centers. Contact your local FSC for further information.

Army Career and Alumni Program (ACAP)

The Army Career and Alumni Program (ACAP) is the principal program the Army offers to assist you in transitioning to your next career. Funded by the Departments of Defense and Army, this program provides a wealth of free, high-quality transition assistance services to all active duty separating or retiring soldiers and their family members. Congressional law and Army policy require that you visit your supporting ACAP office prior to separating to ensure you are aware of your transition services and benefits.

ACAP's mission is to provide you with timely and effective transition assistance. To accomplish its mission, ACAP operates centers at major installations around the world. Check out their website, www.acap.army.mil, which has been significantly enhanced.

You are required to attend an ACAP pre-separation briefing no less than 90 days prior to your leaving the Army. During this briefing, you will learn about your career options, transition benefits, and available services. In addition, you will complete DD Form 2648 (Pre-Separation Checklist). The completed form will serve as your Individual Transition Plan and enable an ACAP counselor to refer you to "service providers," consistent with the transition services you requested on the Pre-Separation Checklist. Finally, you will be counseled on how the Verification of Military Experience and Training document (DD Form 2586) can be used to your advantage during the job search.

Following the briefings and group transition counseling, you will have an opportunity to access the full range of ACAP services. Through your local ACAP center you can:

- Participate in one- to three-day group workshops, which emphasize the development of your job search skills.
- Receive job assistance counseling in the areas of informational interviews, networking, resumes and cover letters, salary negotiation strategies, and more.
- Gain access to a wide array of automated resources, including: resume and cover letter software, the TurboTAP website (www.TurboTAP.org), ACAP Job Opportunities (database of current job vacancies listed by industry and occupation), and other online sites including USA Jobs (www.usajobs.opm.gov/), which presents you with federal job opportunities, and the Go Defense website (www.go-defense.com), which lists DoD jobs and connects you with DoD recruiters and advisors.
- Use the center's reference library, which contains publications such as the *Occupational Outlook Handbook* (www.bls.gov/oco/), *O*NET Dictionary of Occupational Titles* (www.dictionary-occupationaltitles.net), Army Regulation 611/601-

201 (contains information on translating military specialty codes to civilian occupations), and Army Credentialing Opportunities Online (Army COOL, https://www.cool.army.mil/).
- Use the self service center, which normally contains a fax machine, photocopier, telephones, and employer literature.

ACAP XXI Training

ACAP XXI is a self-paced, interactive, computer-based training (CBT) system developed by the Department of the Army. Using leading-edge technology, customized programs provide pre-separation guidance, individualized transition planning information, step-by-step job assistance training, practice interviewing, and related transition support to soldiers and their family members. Graphics and animation highlight key topics and systematically guide the user through the training. Each step of ACAP XXI training builds the foundation for a smooth transition, enabling you to conduct your separation activities while maintaining your active duty responsibilities.

ACAP Express

ACAP Express gives you the ability to go online at any time, from any location, to register and receive ACAP services. Using Army Knowledge Online (AKO) to access ACAP Express, you can schedule attendance at events, access job assistance training tutorials, access an automated resume and cover-letter writer, and access ACAP counselors. For more information, visit https://www.acapexpress.army.mil.

Soldier and Family Assistance Centers (SFACs)

The Army's Soldier and Family Assistance Centers (SFACs) are close to the Army Wounded Warrior Battalions and include the services of an ACAP counselor, who provides Army wounded warriors with one-on-one career counseling and job placement assistance.

ACS Employment Readiness Program (ERP)

The Employment Readiness Program (ERP), operated by the Army Community Service (ACS), is an important program providing these services to adult military family members:

- Resume preparation
- Interviewing techniques
- Career counseling
- Job listings
- Job referrals
- Federal application preparation

Transition Assistance Management Program (TAMP)

The Transition Assistance Management Program (TAMP) is the principal program the government offers to assist transitioning sea service personnel in their next career. TAMP provides direct assistance and counseling to all separating or retiring active duty Navy, Marine Corps, and Coast Guard personnel and their families. We recommend taking advantage of the many high quality career transition services offered through this program.

TAMP is a comprehensive program that addresses virtually every aspect of career transition, including counseling on benefits and entitlements, job search assistance, interview skills, automated professional resumes and federal job applications, and family transition skills.

The TAMP program is administered at Fleet and Family Support Centers (FFSCs) at more than 75 naval installations worldwide. Because 50% of all Navy sailors and officers are deployed away from Navy bases at any given time, the Navy transition program divides the responsibilities of the transition function. The TAMP's primary goal is to provide employment assistance and referral services. If your command does not have access to a Fleet and Family Support Center, a Command Career Counselor has been designated by your Commanding Officer to be the Transition Assistance Program Manager. Personnel on deployed ships and squadrons will need to consult with their Command Career Counselor at least 90 days prior to separation.

TAMP programs provide a wealth of services beyond the career transition services discussed above. Through the FFSCs, sea servicemembers and their spouses can receive assistance in various areas, including relocation, financial and family matters, and retirement benefits. The education, housing, military personnel, transportation management, and chaplain's offices assist separatees with guidance, counseling, and information on career awareness, college and vocational training, moving and storage, and separation benefits. The Departments of Labor and Veterans Affairs offer Transition Assistance Program (TAP) seminars and counsel transitioning military on veterans' benefits at numerous sites throughout the United States. Department of Labor-approved TAP seminars are presented at all overseas bases.

In the Marine Corps, Unit Commanders are responsible for ensuring that all separating Marines are offered initial pre-separation counseling. Marines with at least 180 days of continuous military service are required to attend a Pre-separation Brief at least 90, but preferably 180 days, prior to separation. This mandatory one-day session is organized by transition centers. Marines gain access to these services through their Career Resource Management Centers (CRMCs). Initial contact is with a Career Retention Specialist.

In the Coast Guard, the career transition services are administered through the Work-Life Staffs located at Integrated Support Commands and the Headquarters Support Command. Transition/Relocation Managers assigned to the Work-Life Staffs manage these programs.

Fleet and Family Support Center / Community Services

While TAMP provides an overall framework for retiring and separating personnel, most of the programs and services are coordinated through the Navy's Fleet and Family Support Centers, and the Marine Corps' Community Services. By taking advantage of these programs, you can make the most of your career change. Just as networking expands your possible range of job contacts, taking advantage of all of these programs expands your horizons as well.

The Navy's Fleet and Family Support Centers provide career and job search workshops, counseling and contacts with employers, education and volunteer resources in the communities they serve. They also maintain job banks and referrals on positions in the private and federal sectors. Some offices provide access to a reference library, automated resume writer, personal computers, and copying equipment to assist in job search preparation. Be sure to inquire about personal counseling, which is available at many locations, although service is determined by size of the population and the staff available.

Separatees may continue to use these programs for 90 days after the last day of service. Retirees can take advantage of these programs at any time for as long as necessary. The Department of Defense Transition Bulletin Board and the DoD Job Search website are two of the computerized services available through the Fleet and Family Support Centers. Information on all of these programs can be found later in this chapter.

Contact your local Fleet and Family Support Center (Navy) or Community Services (Marine Corps) at least 90 days prior to separation to access the following services:

- **Employment Workshops:** These workshops include: Job Search Strategies, Resume Writing, Interview Techniques, Owning Your Own Business, Federal Careers Workshops, Career Planning, Job Survival Skills, Job Hunting Skills, Career Dressing Techniques, and many more.
- **Transition and Career Counseling**: Individual career, employment, and transition counseling is available by appointment at all centers.
- **Testing and Assessment:** Two major testing and assessment programs are available to participants—*Discover* and *Strong Interest Inventory*. *Discover* is a self-paced software program available at all sites. An individual can spend hours exploring all areas which range from self-assessment to career information. Alternatively, you can use the system to research a specific college program. *Strong Interest Inventory* assesses your occupational interests.
- **Resume Writer:** A computerized resume writing program.
- **Service Member Occupational Conversion and Training Act:** This program helps relate your military experience to civilian jobs. To be eligible for training, members must either be unemployed for eight out of 15 weeks prior to application, have a military occupation that is not readily transferable to the private sector, or be 30% or more disabled. Training is accomplished through employer-sponsored, VA-approved training plans. Participating employers agree to hire individuals following completion of training. For further information, contact the local Job Service office or VA Regional Office. The VA's number is 1-800-827-1000.
- **Transition Opportunities System (TOPPS):** TOPPS is a computerized program that converts Military Occupational Specialties (MOS) and Naval Enlisted Codes (NEC) to civilian occupations. It also provides unemployment rates and employment trends.
- **Job Club:** An information and networking group can be found in most Fleet and Family Support Centers.
- **Job Information Center:** The Job Information Center is a resource center containing labor market information. Through the Job Information Center you can obtain federal, state, and local area job listings.

Coast Guard Programs

The cornerstone of the U.S. Coast Guard's transition programs are the Transition/Relocation Managers located within the Work-Life Staffs. The Transition/Relocation Managers conduct both the Retirement and Separation Seminars and assist members on an individual basis.

The Separation Seminars are four- to five-day seminars and are offered to all personnel approaching their separation/retirement dates. Ideally, separating members should attend the seminars a minimum of six months before the end of their commitment. Transition Assistance seminars deal with the following topics:

- Transition Counseling
- Basic Resume Writing
- Interviewing Techniques
- Career Dressing
- Basic Job Hunting Skills
- VA Benefits Earned for Military Service
- Social Security Benefits
- Unemployment Benefits
- Travel/Transportation
- Relocation Planning
- Reenlistment Information
- Information on Reserves

- Board of Correction of Military Records
- Discharge Review Board
- Legal Assistance

In addition to the services listed above, the seminar may also include:

- Retired Pay
- Dual Compensation Laws
- Foreign Employment
- Survivor Benefit Plan
- Home of Selection
- Medical Benefits
- Paperwork Processing
- Veterans Group Life Insurance (VGLI)
- Disability Compensation
- VA Education Benefits
- Burial Benefits
- ID Cards
- Processing Point
- VA Retirement Benefits

Anyone wishing to attend a seminar should contact the Transition/Relocation Manager located in the Work-Life Staffs. Phone: 1-800-USCG-WLS (1-800-872-4957) You will hear a recording that will request a three-digit code extension:

Integrated Support Command

Location	Extension
Boston	301
St. Louis	302
Portsmouth	305
Miami	307
New Orleans	308
Cleveland	309
San Pedro	311
Alameda	252
Seattle	313
Honolulu	314
Ketchikan	317
Kodiak	563

Headquarters Support Command

Location	Extension
Cape May	629
Washington, DC	932

In addition to registering for seminars, you may use the 800 number to contact your local center directly and speak with a member of the Work-Life Staff.

Spouse Employment Assistance Program (SEAP)

The Spouse Employment Assistance Program (SEAP) is an integral part of the Fleet and Family Support Center and an important service provider to TAMP. SEAP has been specifically designed to meet the needs of military spouses. It provides spouses of active duty, retired, and transitioning military, as well as federal civilian employees, with the following services:

- Resume Preparation
- Interviewing Techniques
- Career Counseling
- Job Listings
- Job Referrals

If you wish to use the SEAP services, you should contact the SEAP office at the Fleet and Family Support Center nearest you. If you are in the Coast Guard, contact the Transition/Relocation Manager located at the Work-Life Staff nearest you.

Federal Government Transition Programs and Services

Under the name "Operation Transition," the Department of Defense (DoD) has established a framework for transition programs administered by each of the services. Regardless of your branch of service, you will find programs and services administered to meet your needs.

The Operation Transition message to employers is "*Hire Today's Vets. Because it's Right. Because it's Smart*" while separating members are encouraged to "*Get Connected*" by using automated transition assistance programs and other support services provided by DoD.

DoD is committed to the well-being of the men and women who volunteered to serve our country. DoD has implemented an extensive array of services and benefits designed to equip separating servicemembers with the basic job hunting skills, tools, and self-confidence necessary to secure successful employment in the civilian workforce.

Each military service, in conjunction with the Department of Defense, Department of Labor, Department of Veterans Affairs, and state employment service agencies, has initiated innovative transition program components to assist separating military members, civilians, and their families. Each service's program provides counseling in many areas. Pre-separation counseling benefits for participants include:

- Educational benefits, such as the Post-9/11 GI Bill and the Montgomery GI Bill; see http://www.gibill.va.gov/
- An explanation of the procedures for and advantages of, affiliating with the selected Reserve.
- Information concerning government and private sector programs for job search and job placement assistance.
- Employment counseling for spouses.
- Information concerning the availability of relocation assistance services.
- Information concerning the availability of medical and dental coverage following separation from active duty and the opportunity to elect the conversion health policy.
- Information on Public and Community Service.
- Counseling for the servicemember and dependents on the effect of career changes on the individual and his or her family members.
- Financial planning assistance.
- For those being medically separated or retired, a review of the compensation and benefits to which the member may be entitled will be provided from the Department of Veterans Affairs.

Additional benefits (e.g., extended health care) are provided to those members and their families who qualify as involuntary separatees under Public Law 101-510.

DoD transition support and services are vital to ensure that the quality of life remains high for military personnel, even as they prepare to leave military service and embark on new careers. This common sense approach to military separation is the final phase of the new military life cycle. Innovative, user-friendly automated systems are a vital component of DoD sponsored transition services, which include:

The Official Transition Program Website

The DoD Job Search and related America's Job Bank have now been replaced with a new super-charged gateway website for transitioning military, veterans, and their spouses: www.TurboTAP.org. Sponsored by the U.S. Department of Defense, U.S. Department of Labor, and the U.S. Department of Veterans Affairs, this site is rich with resources appropriate for servicemembers, including members of the Guard and Reserve. Be sure to visit this site for all kinds of job assistance, from tips on how to write a military-to-civilian resume and interview for a job to information on civilian occupations, job fairs, certification requirements, licensed occupations, federal government jobs, relocation, and recommended websites. You can also post your resume online and search for job vacancies.

DoD Career Decision Toolkit

The Department of Defense, Department of Labor, Department of Veterans Affairs, and the Services' Transition Assistance Program Working Groups have designed the Career Decision Toolkit to assist servicemembers and their families who are separating, demobilizing or retiring. These services are also available to recovering wounded warriors and their families to effectively plan for the future. The theme of the Career Decision Toolkit is "Goal, Plan and Succeed" (GPS). The Toolkit is designed to guide transitioning servicemembers as they navigate their course to civilian employment and educational opportunities. It is a GPS for success. This Toolkit represents an iterative step in the evolution of providing job search assistance to departing Warriors as they re-enter civilian life.

Public and Community Services (PACS)

The Secretary of Defense is required to encourage and assist separating or retiring military personnel to enter public or community service jobs. This requires establishment of two registries: (1) a "Registry of Public and Community Service Organizations" containing information on organizations interested in hiring former military members, and (2) a "Personnel Registry" of former and separating servicemembers who desire employment in public and community service occupations. DoD counsels separating servicemembers on applying for positions with public and community service organizations.

Verification of Military Experience and Training (VMET)

The Verification of Military Experience and Training (VMET) documents provided to all separating servicemembers translate military skills and training into equivalent civilian experience. A VMET document (DD Form 2586) is provided to all eligible departees to verify their military experience, training history, associated civilian equivalent job title(s), and recommended educational credit information. This helps servicemembers verify previous experience and training for potential employers, write their resumes, interview for jobs, negotiate credits at schools, and obtain certificates or licenses.

Military-to-Civilian Skills Translator

The Department of Labor has an excellent military-to-civilian skills translator, known as O*NET Online, which can be found at http://online.onetcenter.org/crosswalk. The Department of Defense offers Army COOL (https://www.cool.army.mil/search.htm) and Navy COOL (https://www.cool.navy.mil/), both of which will help you find civilian credentials related to your military occupation and training.

If you're unsure as to which civilian occupations are best suited for the skills you developed in the military, these are good websites to start your research.

Veterans Counselors Overseas

DoD, with the support of the VA and DoL, provides separating servicemembers with veterans' services and counseling to the European and Asian theaters.

Troops to Teachers

The Troops to Teachers (TTT) Program, operated by the Defense Activity for Non-Traditional Education Support (DANTES), assists military personnel in starting new careers in public education. The goal of the TTT Program is to help improve American education by providing mature, motivated, experienced, and dedicated personnel for the nation's classrooms. Military personnel entering public education as teachers help relieve teacher shortages, especially in "high-need" schools, and provide positive role models for the nation's public school students. Those interested in elementary or secondary teaching positions must have a bachelor's degree or higher from an accredited college. Those interested in teaching vocational subjects are required to have the equivalent of one year of college and six years of related experience. If interested, contact your base Education Center for an application or download an application from the TTT home page.

Troops to Teachers State Support Offices have been established in over 25 states to assist participants with certification requirements and employment leads. The TTT home page includes a job referral system to allow participants to search for job vacancies as well as links to state Departments of Education, model resumes, other job listings in public education, and other pertinent information. For more information on this program and a listing of state offices, contact:

Defense Activity for Non-Traditional Educational Support (DANTES)
6490 Saufley Field Road
Pensacola, FL 32509-5243
(800) 452-6616 DSN 922-1320
Home Page: www.ProudToServeAgain.com
E-mail: ttt@navy.mil

Department of Labor's Transition Assistance Program (TAP)

The Department of Labor's Transition Assistance Program (TAP) Workshop is a three- to four-day seminar available to all separating military and spouses (on a space-available basis), covering skills assessment, resume preparation, interviewing skills, "dress for success," salary negotiations, military benefits, and other topics designed to facilitate a smooth transition from the military to the civilian community. In addition, military personnel leaving the Armed Forces with service-connected disabilities receive additional help through the Disabled Transition Assistance Program (see below).

The TAP Workshop was established by DoL and is sponsored by the Departments of Labor, Veterans Affairs, and Defense. It is administered by the Veterans Employment and Training Service (VETS) Office in the DoL. The program uses DoL/VETS personnel at the local and state levels or contractors. All separating and retiring servicemembers and their spouses are eligible to attend. The workshops include information on conducting a successful job search, career decision making, evaluating employment options, skills assessment, and veterans benefits.

The DoL TAP Workshops are held at military installations throughout the continental U.S. and at Community Services. Check with your local Transition Assistance Program office for the location of the course nearest you. When you register, be sure to indicate whether you are registering your spouse as well.

Disabled Transition Assistance Program

This program provides servicemembers who are separating or retiring for medical reasons with specialized assistance to learn about VA's Vocational Rehabilitation Program and how to apply. Most sites add a half day onto a TAP workshop for these VA-led sessions.

For veterans enrolled in the VA Vocational Rehabilitation Program, VA pays all tuition, books, fees, and necessary supplies. Training may include college, apprenticeships, or OJT.

Federal Jobs for Veterans

The Veterans Readjustment Appointment (VRA) authority provides veterans with jobs in the federal government. The VRA authority allows federal agencies to appoint Vietnam-era or post Vietnam-era veterans to jobs without competition. Such appointments may lead to conversion to career employment upon satisfactory work for two years.

The Office of Personnel Management (OPM) has developed a useful veterans' guide to federal employment; see http://www.opm.gov/staffingPortal/Vetguide.asp. In addition, the Department of Labor's FirstGov for Workers website, www.firstgov.gov, provides many useful links to major federal job centers and government agencies.

Veterans interested in federal employment should also contact the Human Resources offices of the agencies in which they are interested. To view the list of the program managers responsible for encouraging military recruiting within their respective agencies, visit www. FedsHireVets.gov/AgencyDirectory/index.aspx. Information may also be obtained by contacting any OPM service center by calling USA Jobs by Phone at (478) 757-3000 or visiting www.usajobs.gov. Other good sites include: Federal Jobs Central (www.fedjobs.com), FedWorld (www.fedworld.gov) and Federal Jobs Digest (www.jobsfed.com).

OPM also administers the Disabled Veterans Affirmative Action Program. All federal departments and agencies are required to establish plans to facilitate the recruitment and advancement of disabled veterans. Individuals who are disabled or who served during certain periods have preference in federal jobs. This preference includes additional points for passing exams, consideration for certain jobs, and preference in job retention.

State Government Employment Programs

Most military transition assistance offices can access each state's employment programs, which may include a computerized occupational program and job listings.

Veterans receive special consideration and priority for referral, testing, and counseling from state employment offices, which provide many additional services:

- **Veterans Employment and Training Service Offices:** Within each state's employment services office, you will find Local Veterans' Employment Representatives (LVERs) and Disabled Veterans' Outreach Program (DVOP) specialists who are trained to help you find local job opportunities. They monitor and oversee veterans' employment services, administer veterans' training programs under the Job Training Partnership Act, and protect the reemployment rights of veterans. These representatives can assist veterans with any employment problem. A helpful website to find these state employment offices is located at www.careeronestop.org/MilitaryTransition/.
- **Training opportunities:** Seminars on resume writing, interviewing skills, career changes; information on vocational training; proficiency tests in typing.
- **Information:** State training, employment, and apprenticeship programs, statistics regarding employment availability, economic climate, and cost-of-living data.

Military Associations

As a transitioning servicemember, you have the opportunity to join a variety of military associations, many of which offer some form of job search assistance. Being a member of such an association significantly expands your opportunity to network with other veterans, many of whom are employed in the private sector. We encourage you to join one or more of these associations.

Military Officers Association of America (www.moaa.org) provides an outstanding transition service called TOPS (The Officer Placement Service). It offers a wide range of career transition services to active, former, and retired military officers. To use the services of TOPS, you must be a member of MOAA. Call (800) 245-8762 or (703) 838-8117; www.moaa.org/tops; e-mail: msc@moaa.org.

Non Commissioned Officers Association (www.ncoausa.org) offers the Veterans Employment Assistance (VEA) Program free to military members, retirees, veterans, Guard and Reserve, and their family members. While those who are eligible are encouraged to support NCOA by becoming a member, there is no membership requirement to receive Veterans Employment Assistance. Phone: (210) 653-6161. Address: NCOA, Veterans Employment Assistance Program, P.O. Box 33610, San Antonio, TX 78265.

Reserve Enlisted Association (REA) was formed by enlisted reservists to focus solely on issues affecting enlisted reservists - all ranks, all services - and their families. As mission demands continue to increase and activations become longer and more frequent, REA is working hard to bring attention and equity to quality-of-life areas such as Pay, Retirement, Employment Benefits and Protection, Healthcare, and Education. Your membership support will ensure REA's effectiveness and success. To join REA, visit https://www.reaus.org/membership.html.

Reserve Officers Association's mission is to support and promote the development and execution of a military policy that will provide adequate national security. For its members, ROA provides a wide range of professional and personal benefits including professional development workshops, mentoring programs, and a career center to meet the unique needs of its members. Reserve, active, retired, and former officers and warrant officers of the uniformed services of the U.S. may join ROA by visiting: www.roa.org/.

The Air Force Association (AFA) is an independent, nonprofit aerospace association that represents all elements of the Air Force—officer and enlisted, active and retired, reserve and Air National Guard, cadet and veteran, civil service and CAP, plus anyone who supports the nation's aerospace needs.

In addition to insurance programs and other benefits, AFA offers a resume assistance service. Its team of professional resume writers will prepare a new resume for you or critique an existing one. For more information on AFA, contact:

1501 Lee Highway
Arlington, VA 22209
(800) 727-3337 or (703) 247-5800
www.afa.org
Membership fee: $36 per year; Resume Critique: $50;
Resume Preparation: $160

The **Air Force Aid Society (AFAS)** was established in 1941 in recognition of the fact that as U.S. military personnel were deployed to the European and Pacific theaters, their families back in the States could have difficulty making ends meet. From an initial endowment of $2 million, the fund has grown to over $100 million.

AFAS provides short-term emergency financial assistance to active duty Air Force personnel and their families. Assistance ranges from repairs on essential transportation to funds for food, funeral expenses, and emergency travel. AFAS assistance is available 24 hours a day, seven days a week. To obtain AFAS assistance, contact your local FSC (www.afas.org).

Association of the United States Army (AUSA) offers a free transition booklet titled, *Once a Soldier, Always a Soldier—Getting Ready to Retire*. For further information on membership and services, contact:

Association of the United States Army
2425 Wilson Boulevard
Arlington, VA 22201
(800) 336-4570 or (703) 841-4300; Fax: (703) 841-7570
www.ausa.org
$20-38 annually depending on grade. Special $12 dues for junior enlisted members (E-1 to E-4)

U.S. Army Warrant Officers Association (USAWAO) is open to active Army, National Guard, Reserve, retired, and former Warrant Officers. The association fosters a spirit of patriotism among its members, recommends programs for improvement of the Army, disseminates professional information among Warrant Officers, and promotes comradeship among its members. For more about USAWAO, visit www.usawoa.org.

Navy League of the United States (www.NavyLeague.org) is a powerful voice for strong maritime commitment: Navy, Marine Corps, Coast Guard, and Merchant Marines. The Navy League's missions include 300 Councils directly supporting active duty sea service personnel and families; educating the nation's leaders and nation; building America's future through the Naval Sea Cadet Corps and scholarships, and the Hiring Center's (www.NavyLeague.org) career matching service. Membership is open to veterans, civilians, and active duty seas servicemembers and spouses. Address: 2300 Wilson Boulevard, Suite 200, Arlington, VA 22201-3308; Call: (703) 528-1775; toll-free: (800) 356-5760.

Fleet Reserve Association (www.fra.org) is open to all enlisted personnel (active duty, reserve, and retired) of the U.S. Navy, Marine Corps, and Coast Guard. Transitioning members will value the access to Nationwide Resumes of America. Nationwide Resumes of America offers members assistance in preparing resumes. Call: (800) FRA-1924 or (703) 683-1400. Address: Fleet Reserve Association, 125 N. West Street, Alexandria, VA 22314-9765.

Marine Executive Association (www.marineea.org) provides assistance in the job market to those Marines transitioning from active to reserve or retired status.

Marine Corps Reserve Association (www.usmcra.org) provides transition information to active and retired Reserve Marines through a range of publications and services. Call: (703) 630-3772. Address: MCRA, 8626 Lee Highway, Fairfax, VA 22031.

Marine Corps League (www.mcleague.org) is open to those currently serving in the United States Marine Corps or those who have been honorably discharged or retired. The League provides services and activities in many communities. Call: (703) 207-9588; (800) MCL-1775. Membership: $30.

Marine for Life (http://www.m4l.usmc.mil/) connects Marines with other Marines who can assist in the job search. Free service.

Armed Forces Communications and Electronics Association (www.afcea.org) provides its members with a range of transition services, including: career transition seminars, Resume Preparation Guide, and a Career Transition Handbook. Membership is open to members of any rank. Call: (800) 336-4583 or (703) 631-6100. Address: AFCEA, 4400 Fair Lakes Court, Fairfax, VA 22033. Membership: $35 annually or $85 for three years.

American Legion (www.legion.org) is the world's largest veterans' organization. Their prime objective is the care and support of veterans.

Veterans of Foreign Wars (www.vfw.org) is a strong voice for veterans and a catalyst for change in improving veterans' benefits.

Disabled American Veterans (www.dav.org) provides aid to those veterans disabled during time of war or armed conflict.

To view a compiled list of free career transition services. visit www.CorporateGray.com and click on the Transition Guide tab.

chapter 4

Identify Your Skills, Interests, and Values

WHAT SKILLS DO YOU POSSESS that are most relevant to today's job market? Are the skills you acquired in the military attractive to many employers? What other skills do you possess which may or may not be related to your work in the military? Do you need to acquire new skills?

We live in a skills-based society where individuals market their skills to employers in exchange for money, position, and power. The ease by which individuals change jobs and careers is directly related to their ability to communicate their skills to employers and then transfer their skills to new work settings.

To best position yourself in the job markets of today and tomorrow, you should pay particular attention to refining your present skills as well as achieving new and more marketable skills. This may mean going back to school for a degree or certificate or taking advantage of employer-sponsored training programs.

Military to Civilian Skills

But before you can refine your skills or acquire additional skills, you need to know what skills you presently possess. What skills did you acquire in the military that are directly transferable to the civilian work world? Unfortunately, few people can identify and talk about their skills even though they possess numerous skills which they use on a regular basis. This becomes a real problem when they must write a resume or go to a job interview. Since employers want to know about your specific abilities and skills, you must learn to both identify and communicate your skills to employers. You should be able to explain what it is you do well and give examples relevant to employers' needs.

What skills do you already have to offer employers? Regardless of what you did while in the service, we're confident that after reading this chapter you'll be able to identify several transferable skills based on your military experience. Will that be enough? It depends. If the employment field in which you are interested requires specific work-content skills that you do not possess, then the answer is no. If, however, no specific work-content skills are required and the prospective employer thinks that you can be trained, then the answer is yes.

Civilian Credentialing

Regardless of whether or not you have a college degree, you have gained experience through your military service. Now may be a good time to take stock of what you have and what you need to pursue a civilian career. Depending on your circumstances, it may make more sense for you to pursue a certificate or earn civilian credentials in your field. To assist you in identifying civilian credentialing requirements, visit Credentialing Opportunities On-Line (COOL) for the Army and Navy: www.cool.army.mil and www.cool.navy.mil. Also, check out the credentialing sections of America's Career Information Network (www.ACINet.org), America's CareerOneStop (Workforce Credentialing Information Center—www.careeronestop.org), GoArmyEd (www.goarmyed.com), and DANTES (www.dantes.doded.mil).

> Now would be a good time to take stock of the skills you have and the skills you need.

For those of you who decide that now is a good time to obtain your bachelor's or master's degree, you'll have to decide whether you want to do it on a part-time or full-time basis. Such a decision requires much forethought. If you do make the investment in time now to pursue this degree, how will it increase your income potential 5, 15, or 25 years from now? Are you able financially to go to school full time or would it make more sense to find full-time employment immediately and then pursue your bachelor's or advanced degree on a part-time basis? Only you know the answers to these questions.

If you have just completed an educational program relevant to today's job market, the skills you have to offer are most likely related to the subject matter you studied. As you transition from the military, the skills you wish to communicate to employers will most likely be those you have already demonstrated in specific military jobs. If your degree or certificate is in the same area, you can use it as a leverage to increase your market value to a prospective employer. If, on the other hand, the degree or certificate is in a totally different area, you can honestly claim to have received academic training in this particular discipline. Depending on your circumstances, it may be worthwhile to find temporary employment in that area on an interim basis so that you can later truthfully claim to have both educational training and work experience in your desired field of employment.

The skills required for finding a job are no substitute for the skills necessary for doing the job. Learning new skills requires a major investment of time, money, and effort. Nonetheless, the long-term pay-off should more than justify the initial costs. Indeed, research continues to show that well selected education and training provide the best returns on individual and societal investment. Be sure you well understand and take advantage of the excellent educational benefits you earned through your military service. Many who have traveled the road before you know that education is the key to success. We encourage you to unlock the secrets of your potential.

Types of Skills

Most people possess two types of skills that define their accomplishments and strengths as well as enable them to enter and advance within the job market: work-content skills and functional skills. You need to acquaint yourself with these skills before communicating them to employers.

We assume you have already acquired certain **work-content skills** necessary to function effectively in today's job market. These "hard skills" are easy to recognize since they are often identified as "qualifications" for specific jobs; they are the subject of most educational and training programs. Work-content skills tend to be technical and job-specific in nature. Examples of such skills include helicopter repair, programming computers, teaching history, or operating an X-ray machine. They may require formal training, are associated with specific trades or professions, and are used only in certain job and career settings. One uses a separate skills vocabulary, jargon, and subject matter for specifying technical qualifications of individuals entering and advancing in an occupation. While these skills do not transfer well from one occupation to another, they are critical for entering and advancing within certain occupations.

At the same time, you possess numerous **functional/transferable skills** employers readily seek along with your work-content skills. These "soft" skills are associated with numerous job settings, are mainly acquired through experience rather than formal training, and can be communicated through a general vocabulary. Functional/transferable skills are less easy to recognize since they tend to be linked to certain personal characteristics (energetic, intelligent, likable) and the ability to deal with processes (communicate, solve problems, motivate) rather than do things (build a house, repair air conditioners). While most people have only a few work-content skills, they may have numerous—as many as 300—functional/transferable skills. These skills enable job seekers to more easily change jobs. But you must first know your functional skills before you can relate them to the job market.

Assess your functional and work-content skills before you decide you need training.

Most people view the world of work in traditional occupational job skill terms. This is a structural view of occupational realities. Occupational fields are seen as consisting of separate and distinct jobs which, in turn, require specific work-content skills. From this perspective, occupations and jobs are relatively self-contained entities. Social work, for example, is seen as being different from paralegal work; social workers, therefore, are not "qualified" to seek paralegal work.

On the other hand, a functional view of occupations and jobs emphasizes the similarity of job characteristics as well as common linkages between different occupations. Although the structure of occupations and jobs may differ, they have similar functions. They involve working with people, data, processes, and objects. If you work with people, data, processes, and objects in one occupation, you can transfer that experience to other occupations which have similar functions. Once you understand how your skills relate to the functions as well as investigate the structure of different occupations, you should be prepared to make job changes from one occupational field to another. Whether you possess the necessary work-content skills to qualify for entry into the other occupational field is another question altogether.

The skills we identify and help you organize in this chapter are the functional skills career counselors normally emphasize when advising clients to assess their strengths. In contrast to work-content skills, functional skills can be transferred from one job or career to another. They enable individuals to make some job and career changes without acquiring additional education and training. They constitute an important bridge for moving from one occupation to another.

Before you decide if you need more education or training, you should first assess both your functional and work-content skills to see how they can be transferred to other jobs and occupations. Once you do this, you should be better prepared to communicate your qualifications to employers with a rich skills-based vocabulary.

Your Strengths

Regardless of what combination of work-content and functional skills you possess, a job search must begin with identifying your strengths. Without knowing these, your job search will lack content and focus. After all, your goal should be to find a job that is fit for you rather than one you think you might be able to fit into. Of course, you also want to find a job for which there is a demand. This particular focus requires a well-defined approach to identifying and communicating your skills to others. You can best do this by asking the right questions about your strengths and then conducting a systematic self-assessment of what you do best. The counselors in the career transition offices are skilled in helping you identify the functional and work-content skills you possess. We caution you not to sell yourself short. Regardless of which branch you served, we know that you gained experience in many areas. Now your challenge is to identify those skills by asking the right questions.

Ask the Right Questions

Knowing the right questions to ask will save you time and steer you into productive job search channels from the very beginning. Asking the wrong questions can cripple your job search efforts and leave you frustrated. The questions must be understood from the perspectives of both employers and applicants.

Two of the most humbling questions you will encounter in your job search are "Why should I hire you?" and "What are your weaknesses?" While employers may not directly ask these questions, they are asking them nonetheless. If you can't answer these questions in a positive manner—directly, indirectly, verbally, or nonverbally—your job search will likely flounder and you will join the ranks of the unsuccessful and disillusioned job searchers who feel something is wrong with them. Individuals who have lost their jobs are particularly vulnerable to these questions since many have lowered self-esteem and self-image as a result of the job loss. Many such people focus on what is wrong rather than what is right about themselves. Such thinking creates self-fulfilling prophecies and is self-destructive in the job market. By all means avoid such negative thinking.

Employers want to hire your value or strengths—not your weaknesses. Since it is easier to identify and interpret weaknesses, employers look for indicators of your strengths by identifying your weaknesses. The more successful you are in communicating your strengths, the better off you will be in relation to both employers and fellow applicants.

Unfortunately, many people work against their own best interests. Not knowing their strengths, they market their weaknesses by first identifying job vacancies and then trying to fit their "qualifications" into job descriptions. This approach often frustrates applicants; it presents a picture of a job market which is not interested in the applicant's strengths. This leads some people toward acquiring new skills which they hope will be marketable, even though they do not enjoy using them. Millions of individuals find themselves in such misplaced situations. Your task is to avoid joining the ranks of the misplaced and unhappy workforce by first understanding your skills and then relating them to your interests and goals. In so doing, you will be in a better position to target your job search toward jobs that should become especially rewarding and fulfilling.

Functional/Transferable Skills

We know that many people stumble into jobs by accident. Some are at the right place at the right time to take advantage of a job or career opportunity. Others work hard at trying to fit into jobs listed in classified ads, employment agencies, and personnel offices; identified through friends and acquaintances; or found by knocking on doors. After 15 to 20 years in the work world, many people wish they had better planned their careers from the very start. All of a sudden they are unhappily locked into jobs because of retirement benefits and the family responsibilities of raising children and meeting monthly mortgage payments.

After 10 to 15 years of work experience, most people have a good idea of what they like and don't like to do. While their values are more set than when they first began working, many people are still unclear as to what they do well and how their skills fit into the job market. What other jobs, for example, might they be qualified to perform? If they have the opportunity to change jobs or careers—either voluntarily or involuntarily—and find the time to plan the change, they can move into jobs and careers which fit their skills.

The key to understanding your non-technical strengths is to identify your transferable or functional skills. Once you have done this, you will be better prepared to identify what it is you want to do. Moreover, your self-image and self-esteem will improve. Better still, you will be prepared to communicate your strengths to others through a rich skills-based vocabulary. These outcomes are critically important for writing your resume and letters as well as for conducting informational and job interviews.

Let's illustrate the concept of functional/transferable skills. Suppose that you are a Non Commissioned Officer. Many NCOs view their skills in strict work-content terms—knowledge, use, and maintenance of a weapon system. When looking for jobs in the civilian world, these individuals know that they will find very few jobs that will allow them to directly build on this type of expertise. Instead, they must rely on the wealth of other skills they have acquired while in the service to help them find suitable employment. Examples of these skills that are directly transferable to business and industry include:

- leadership
- discipline
- self-confidence
- teaching ability
- interpersonal skills
- writing
- perseverance
- general knowledge
- insight
- multicultural perspective
- critical thinking
- imagination

Most functional/transferable skills can be classified into two general skills and trait categories—organizational/interpersonal skills and personality/work style traits:

Types of Transferable Skills (Figure 4-1)

Organizational and Interpersonal Skills

__	communicating	__	trouble-shooting
__	problem solving	__	implementing
__	analyzing/assessing	__	self-understanding
__	planning	__	understanding
__	decision-making	__	setting goals
__	innovating	__	conceptualizing
__	thinking logically	__	generalizing
__	evaluating	__	managing time
__	identifying problems	__	creating
__	synthesizing	__	judging
__	forecasting	__	controlling
__	tolerating ambiguity	__	organizing
__	motivating	__	persuading
__	leading	__	encouraging
__	selling	__	improving
__	performing	__	designing
__	reviewing	__	consulting
__	attaining	__	teaching
__	team building	__	cultivating
__	updating	__	advising
__	coaching	__	training
__	supervising	__	interpreting
__	estimating	__	achieving
__	negotiating	__	reporting
__	administering	__	managing

Personality and Work Style Traits

__	diligent	__	honest
__	patient	__	reliable
__	innovative	__	perceptive
__	persistent	__	assertive
__	tactful	__	sensitive
__	loyal	__	astute
__	successful	__	risk taker
__	versatile	__	easygoing
__	enthusiastic	__	calm
__	outgoing	__	flexible
__	expressive	__	competent
__	adaptable	__	punctual
__	democratic	__	receptive
__	resourceful	__	diplomatic
__	determining	__	self-confident
__	creative	__	tenacious
__	open	__	discrete
__	objective	__	talented
__	warm	__	empathetic
__	orderly	__	tidy
__	tolerant	__	candid
__	frank	__	adventuresome
__	cooperative	__	firm
__	dynamic	__	sincere
__	self-starter	__	initiator
__	precise	__	competent
__	sophisticated	__	diplomatic
__	effective	__	efficient

These are the types of skills you need to identify and then communicate to employers in your resume and letters as well as during interviews. This skills vocabulary helps you better translate your military work experience into civilian occupational language.

Identify Your Skills

If you were just graduating from high school or college and did not know what you wanted to do, we would recommend that you take a battery of vocational tests and psychological inventories to identify your interests and skills. Since you are leaving the military, you don't fall into these categories of job seekers, chances are you don't need complex testing. You have experience, you have well defined values, and you know what you don't like in a job. Nonetheless, check with your local military transition assistance center to see if they administer assessment tests. Such tests can provide you with a solid base of information on yourself for organizing and implementing an effective job search.

We outline several alternative paper-and-pencil skills identification exercises—from simple to complex—for assisting you at this stage. We recommend using the Motivated Skills Exercise in Chapter 5 to gain a thorough understanding of your strengths.

Use the exercises in this chapter to identify both your work-content and transferable skills. These self-assessment techniques stress your positives or strengths rather than identify your negatives or weaknesses. They should generate a rich vocabulary for communicating your "qualifications" to employers. Each exercise requires different investments of your time and effort as well as varying degrees of assistance from other people.

If you feel these exercises are inadequate for your needs, by all means seek professional assistance from a testing or assessment center staffed by a licensed psychologist. Such centers do in-depth testing which goes further than these self-directed skill exercises.

Checklist Method

This is the simplest method for identifying your strengths. Review the different types of transferable skills outlined in Figure 4-1. Place a "1" in front of the skills that strongly characterize you; assign a "2" to those that describe you to a large extent; put a "3" before those that describe you to some extent. After completing this exercise, review the lists and rank order the 10 characteristics that best describe you on each list.

Autobiography of Accomplishments

Write a lengthy essay about your life accomplishments. This could range from 20 to 100 pages. After completing the essay, go through it page by page to identify what you most enjoyed doing (working with different kinds of information, people, and things) and what skills you used most frequently as well as enjoyed using. Finally, identify those skills you wish to continue using. After analyzing and synthesizing this data, you should have a relatively clear picture of your strongest skills.

Computerized Assessment Systems

While the previous self-directed exercises required you to either respond to checklists of skills or reconstruct and analyze your past job experiences, several computerized self-assessment programs are designed to help individuals identify their skills. Many of the programs are available in schools, colleges, and libraries. Some of the most popular are:

- Career Information System (CIS)
- Career Navigator
- Choices
- Discover II
- Guidance Information System (GIS)
- SIGI-Plus (System of Interactive Guidance and Information)

Most of these comprehensive career planning programs do much more than just assess skills. As we will see in Chapter 5, they also integrate other key components in the career planning process—interests, values, goals, related jobs, college majors, education and training programs, and job search plans. You might check with the career or counseling center at your local community college to see what computerized career assessment systems are available for your use. They are relatively easy to use and they generate a great deal of useful career planning information. Many will print out a useful analysis of how your interests and skills are related to specific jobs and careers.

Interests and Values

Knowing what you do well is essential for understanding your strengths and for linking your capabilities to specific jobs. However, just knowing your abilities and skills will not give your job search the direction it needs for finding the right job. You also need to know your work values and interests. These are the basic building blocks for setting goals and targeting your abilities toward certain jobs and careers.

Take, for example, the Administrative Specialist who types 120 words a minute. While this person possesses a highly marketable skill, if the person doesn't enjoy using this skill and is more interested in working outdoors, this will not become a motivated skill; the individual will most likely not pursue a typing job. Your interests and values will determine whether or not certain skills should play a central role in your job search.

Vocational Interests

We all have interests. Most change over time. Many of your interests may center on your present job whereas others relate to activities that define your hobbies and leisure activities. A good place to start identifying your interests is by examining the information and exercises found in both *The Complete Guide For Occupational Exploration* and *The Enhanced Guide For Occupational Exploration*. Widely used by students and others first entering the civilian job market, it is also relevant to individuals who already have work experience. The guide classifies all jobs in the U.S. into 12 interest areas. Examine the following list of interest areas. In the first column, check those work areas that appeal to you. In the second column, rank order those areas you checked in the first column. Start with "1" to indicate the most interesting:

My Work Interests (Figure 4-2)

Organizational and Interpersonal Skills

Yes (✓)	Ranking (1-12)	Interest Area
____	____	**Artistic:** an interest in creative expression of feelings or ideas.
____	____	**Scientific:** an interest in discovering, collecting, and analyzing information about the natural world, and in applying scientific research findings to problems in medicine, the life sciences, and the natural sciences.
____	____	**Plants and animals:** an interest in working with plants and animals, usually outdoors.
____	____	**Protective:** an interest in using authority to protect people and property.
____	____	**Mechanical:** an interest in applying mechanical principles to practical situations by using machines or hand tools.
____	____	**Industrial:** an interest in repetitive, concrete, organized activities done in a factory setting.
____	____	**Business detail:** an interest in organized, clearly defined activities requiring accuracy and attention to details.
____	____	**Selling:** an interest in bringing others to a particular point of view by personal persuasion, using sales and promotional techniques.
____	____	**Accommodating:** an interest in catering to the wishes and needs of others, usually on a one-to-one basis.
____	____	**Humanitarian:** an interest in helping others with their mental, spiritual, social, physical, or vocational needs.
____	____	**Leading and influencing:** an interest in leading and influencing others by using high-level verbal or numerical abilities.

The *Guide For Occupational Exploration* also includes other checklists relating to home-based and leisure activities that may or may not relate to your work interests. If you are unclear about your work interests, you might want to consult these other interest exercises. You may discover that some of your home-based and leisure activity interests should become your work interests. Indeed, many people turn hobbies or home activities into full-time jobs after deciding that such "work" is what they really enjoy doing. Examples of such interests include:

Leisure and Home-Based Interests

___ Acting in a play or amateur variety show.
___ Advising family members on their personal problems.
___ Announcing or emceeing a program.
___ Applying first aid in emergencies as a volunteer.
___ Building model airplanes, automobiles, or boats.
___ Building or repairing computers.
___ Buying large quantities of food for an organization.
___ Campaigning for political candidates or issues.
___ Canning and preserving food.
___ Carving small wooden objects.
___ Coaching children or youth in sports activities.
___ Conducting house-to-house or telephone surveys for a PTA.
___ Creating or styling hair for friends.
___ Designing your own greeting cards and writing original verses.
___ Developing film.
___ Doing impersonations.
___ Doing public speaking or debating.
___ Entertaining at parties or other events.
___ Helping conduct physical exercises for disabled people.
___ Making ceramic objects.
___ Modeling clothes for a fashion show.
___ Mounting and framing pictures.
___ Nursing sick pets.
___ Painting the interior or exterior of a home.
___ Performing experiments involving plants.
___ Playing a musical instrument.
___ Refinishing or reupholstering furniture.
___ Repairing electrical household appliances.
___ Repairing the family car.
___ Repairing or assembling bicycles.
___ Repairing plumbing in the house.
___ Speaking on radio or television.
___ Taking photographs.
___ Teaching Sunday School
___ Tutoring pupils in school subjects.
___ Weaving rugs or making quilts.
___ Writing articles, stories, or plays.
___ Writing songs for club socials or amateur plays.

For more sophisticated treatments of work interests, which are also validated through testing procedures, contact a career counselor, a county Adult Continuing Education Office, a community college, or a testing and assessment center for information on these tests:

- Strong Interest Inventory
- Myers-Briggs Type Indicator
- Kuder Occupational Interest Survey
- Jackson Vocational Interest Survey
- Vocational Interest Inventory
- Career Assessment Inventory
- Temperament and Values Inventory

Keep in mind that not all testing and assessment instruments used by career counselors are equally valid for career planning purposes. While the Strong Interest Inventory appears to be the most relevant for career decision-making, the Myers-Briggs Type Indicator is also popular. In addition to these professionally administered and interpreted tests, try also Holland's "The Self-Directed Search," found at www.self-directed-search.com.

Work Values

Work values are those attributes you developed on the job; for example, loyalty, dedication, team playing, and ability to work under pressure.

Most jobs involve a combination of likes and dislikes. By identifying what you both like and dislike about jobs, you should be able to better identify jobs that involve tasks that you will most enjoy.

Several exercises can help you identify your work values. First, identify what most satisfies you about work by completing this exercise:

My Work Values (Figure 4-3)

I prefer employment which enables me to:

___	contribute to society	___	be creative
___	have contact with people	___	supervise others
___	work alone	___	work with details
___	work with a team	___	gain recognition
___	compete with others	___	acquire security
___	make decisions	___	make money
___	work under pressure	___	help others
___	use power and authority	___	solve problems
___	acquire new knowledge	___	take risks
___	be a recognized expert	___	work at my own pace

Select four work values from the above list which are the most important to you and list them below. List any other work values (desired satisfactions) which were not listed above but are nonetheless important to you:

1. ______________________________
2. ______________________________
3. ______________________________
4. ______________________________

Another approach to identifying work values is outlined in *The Guide For Occupational Exploration*. In the first column, check those work areas that appeal to you. In the second column, rank order from 1 (highest) to 5 (lowest) the five most important values:

Ranking Work Values (Figure 4-4)

Yes (✓)	Ranking (1-12)	Work Values
____	____	**Adventure:** Working in a job that requires taking risks.
____	____	**Authority:** Working in a job in which you use your position to control others.
____	____	**Competition:** Working in a job in which you compete with others.
____	____	**Creativity and self-expression:** Working in a job in which you use your imagination to find new ways to do or say something.
____	____	**Flexible work schedule:** Working in a job where you choose your work hours.
____	____	**Helping others:** Working in a job in which you provide direct services to persons with problems.
____	____	**High salary:** Working in a job making lots of money.
____	____	**Independence:** Working in a job in which you decide for yourself what work to do and how to do it.
____	____	**Influencing others:** Working in a job in which you influence the opinions or decisions of others.
____	____	**Intellectual stimulation:** Working in a job which requires a great amount of thought and reasoning.
____	____	**Leadership:** Working in a job in which you direct, manage, or supervise the activities of others.
____	____	**Outside work:** Working out-of-doors.
____	____	**Persuading:** Working in a job in which you personally convince others to take certain actions.
____	____	**Physical work:** Working in a job which requires substantial physical activity.
____	____	**Prestige:** Working in a job which gives you status and respect.
____	____	**Public attention:** Working in a job in which you attract immediate notice because of appearance or activity.
____	____	**Public contact:** Working in a job in which you daily deal with the public.
____	____	**Recognition:** Working in a job in which you gain public notice.
____	____	**Research work:** Working in a job in which you discover new facts and develop ways to apply them.
____	____	**Routine work:** Working in a job in which you follow established procedures requiring little change.
____	____	**Seasonal work**: Working in a job in which you are employed only at certain times of the year.
____	____	**Travel:** Working in a job in which you take frequent trips.
____	____	**Variety:** Working in a job in which your duties change frequently.
____	____	**Work with children:** Working in a job in which you teach or care for children.
____	____	**Work with hands:** Working in a job in which you use your hands or hand tools.
____	____	**Work with machines or equipment:** Working in a job in which you use machines or equipment.
____	____	**Work with numbers:** Working in a job in which you use math or statistics.

Second, develop a comprehensive list of your past and present job frustrations and dissatisfactions. This should help you identify negative factors you should avoid in jobs.

My Job Frustrations and Dissatisfactions (Figure 4-5)

List and rank order as many past and present things that frustrate or make you dissatisfied and unhappy in job situations:

1. ______________________________
2. ______________________________
3. ______________________________
4. ______________________________
5. ______________________________

Third, brainstorm "Ten or More Things I Love to Do." Identify which ones could be incorporated into what kinds of work environments. Fourth, list at least 10 things you most enjoy about work and rank each item accordingly Fifth, you should also identify the types of interpersonal environments you prefer working in. Do this by specifying the types of people you like and dislike associating with.

Your Future as Objectives

All of these exercises are designed to explore your past and present work-related values. At the same time, you need to project your values into the future. What, for example, do you want to do over the next 5, 10, or 20 years? We'll return to this type of value question when we address in Chapter 6 the critical objective-setting stage of the job search process.

To further assist you in assessing your skills and interests, visit www.CorporateGray.com and click on the Transition Guide tab. While there, be sure to take the Myers-Briggs Type Indicator.

chapter 5

Know Your Motivated Abilities and Skills

ONCE YOU KNOW WHAT YOU DO well and enjoy doing, you next need to analyze those interests, values, abilities, and skills that form a recurring motivated pattern. This "pattern" is the single most important piece of information you need to know about yourself in the whole self-assessment process. Knowing your skills and abilities alone without knowing how they relate to your interests and values will not give you the necessary direction for finding the job you want. You simply must know your pattern.

What's Your MAS?

The concept of motivated abilities and skills (MAS) enables us to relate your interests and values to your skills and abilities. But how do we identify your MAS beyond the questions and exercises outlined thus far?

Your pattern of motivated abilities and skills becomes evident once you analyze your achievements or accomplishments. For it is your achievements that tell us what you both did well and enjoyed doing. If we analyze and synthesize many of your achievements, we are likely to identify a recurring pattern that most likely goes back to your childhood and which will continue to characterize your achievements in the future.

An equally useful exercise would be to identify your weaknesses by analyzing your failures. These, too, would fall into recurring patterns. Understanding what your weaknesses are might help you avoid jobs and work situations that bring out the worst in you. Indeed, you may learn more about yourself by analyzing your failures than by focusing solely on your accomplishments.

For now, let's focus on your positives rather than your negatives. After you complete the strength exercises in this chapter, you may want to reverse the procedures to identify your weaknesses.

Numerous self-directed exercises can assist you in identifying your pattern of motivated abilities and skills. The basic requirements for making these exercises work for you are time and analytical ability. You must spend a considerable amount of time detailing your achievements by looking at your history of accomplishments. Once you complete the historical reconstruction task, you must comb through your "stories" to identify recurring themes and patterns. This requires a high level of analytical ability which you may or may not possess. If analysis and synthesis are not two of your strong skills, you may want to seek assistance from a friend or professional who is good at analyzing and synthesizing information presented in narrative form. Career counselors in your military transition assistance office can help you.

Several paper and pencil exercises help identify your pattern of motivated abilities and skills. We outline some of the most popular and thorough exercises that have proved useful to thousands of people.

Autobiography of Accomplishments

This exercise requires you to write a lengthy essay about your life accomplishments. Your essay may run anywhere from 20 to 200 pages. After completing it, go through it page by page to identify what aspects of your service experience you most enjoyed (working with different kinds of data, people, processes, and objects) and what skills you used most frequently as well as enjoyed using. Finally, identify those skills you wish to continue using. After analyzing and synthesizing this data, you should have a relatively clear picture of your strongest skills.

This exercise requires a great deal of self-discipline and analytical skill. To do it properly, you must write as much as possible, and in as much detail as possible, about your accomplishments. The richer the detail, the better will be your analysis.

Motivated Skills Exercise

Our final exercise is one of the most complex and time-consuming self-assessment exercises. However, it yields some of the best data on motivated abilities and skills, and it is especially useful for those who feel they need a more thorough analysis of their past achievements. This device is widely used by career counselors. Initially developed by Haldane Associates, this particular exercise is variously referred to as "Success Factor Analysis," "System to Identify Motivated Skills," or "Intensive Skills Identification."

This technique helps you identify which skills you enjoy using. While you can use this technique on your own, it is best to work with someone else. Since you will need six to eight hours to properly complete this exercise, divide your time into two or three work sessions.

The exercise consists of six steps. The steps follow the basic pattern of generating raw data, identifying patterns, analyzing the data through reduction techniques, and synthesizing the patterns into a transferable skills vocabulary. You need strong analytical skills to complete this exercise on your own. The six steps include:

1. **Identify 15-20 achievements:** These consist of things you enjoyed doing, believe you did well, and felt a sense of satisfaction, pride, or accomplishment in doing. You can see yourself performing at your best and enjoying your experiences when you analyze your achievements. This information reveals your motivations since it deals entirely with your voluntary behavior. In addition, it identifies what is right with you by focusing on your positives and strengths. Identify achievements throughout your life, beginning with your childhood and continuing through your present job. You may find it helpful to peruse past fitness or performance reports (OERs/EERs), to readily identify specific military achievements. Your achievements should relate to specific experiences—not general ones—and may be drawn from work, leisure, education, or home life. Put each achievement at the top of a separate sheet of paper. For example, your achievements might appear as follows:

Sample Achievement Statements

"When I first joined the military, I had never fired a weapon. After some good coaching from my NCOs, I scored expert the second time my unit went to the firing range."

"I earned a Bachelor's Degree in Economics from the University of Dayton while serving at Wright Patterson Air Force Base, Ohio. By taking evening courses over a four year period, I was able to satisfy all of the degree requirements and also perform my military duties.

"The proudest day of my life occurred when I completed flight school training. It was the most demanding training I have ever been through."

"Though I was the smallest soldier in the battalion, I won the intramural wrestling title for my weight group three consecutive years."

"As a participant in Operation Enduring Freedom, I will always remember the night our tanker refueled five aircraft in flight over a 4-hour period."

"Leaving a C-130 at night while moving at 150 knots at 1300 feet was one of the greatest experiences of my life."

"Being selected the honor graduate of my F-16 Flight School class."

"I didn't think the Survival and Escape training was worth it until I was captured by Iraq's Revolutionary Guard. In less than three days, I escaped from enemy territory and returned to friendly forces."

2. Prioritize your five most significant achievements.

1. ____
2. ____
3. ____
4. ____
5. ____

3. Write a full page on each of your prioritized achievements. You should describe:

- How you initially became involved.
- The details of what you did and how you did it.
- What was especially enjoyable or satisfying to you.

Use copies of the "Detailing Your Achievements" form (see Figure 5-2) to outline your achievements.

4. **Elaborate on your achievements:** Have one or two other people interview you. For each achievement, have them note on a separate sheet of paper any terms used to reveal your skills, abilities, and personal qualities. To elaborate details, the interviewer(s) may ask:

    - *What was involved in the achievement?*
    - *What was your part?*
    - *What did you actually do?*
    - *How did you go about that?*

    Clarify any vague areas by providing an example or illustration of what you actually did. Have the interviewer probe with the following questions:

    - *Would you elaborate on one example of what you mean?*
    - *Could you give me an illustration?*
    - *What were you good at doing?*

    This interview should clarify the details of your activities by asking only "what" and "how" questions. It should take 45 to 90 minutes to complete.

5. **Identify patterns by examining the interviewer's notes:** Together identify the recurring skills, abilities, and personal qualities demonstrated in your achievements. Search for patterns. Your skills pattern should be clear at this point; you should feel comfortable with it. If you have questions, review the data. If you disagree with a conclusion, disregard it. The results must accurately and honestly reflect how you operate.

6. **Synthesize the information by clustering similar skills into categories:** For example, your skills might be grouped in the following manner:

Synthesized Skill Clusters (Figure 5-1)

Investigate/Survey/Read Inquire/Probe/Question	Teach/Train/Drill Perform/Show/Demonstrate
Learn/Memorize/Practice Evaluate/Appraise/Assess	Construct/Assemble
	Organize/Structure/Provide Definition/Plan/Chart Course/ Strategize/Coordinate
Influence/Involve/Get Participation/Publicize/Promote	Create/Design/Adapt/Modify

Detailing Your Achievements (Figure 5-2)

ACHIEVEMENT # : ____

____

____

____

1. How did I initially become involved? ______________________________

 ____

 ____

 ____

 ____

2. What did I do? ______________________________

 ____

 ____

 ____

 ____

3. How did I do it? ______________________________

 ____

 ____

 ____

 ____

4. What was especially enjoyable about doing it? ______________________________

 ____

 ____

 ____

 ____

This exercise yields a relatively comprehensive inventory of your skills. The information will better enable you to use a skills vocabulary when identifying your objective, writing your resume and letters, and interviewing. Your self-confidence and self-esteem should increase accordingly.

Benefit From Redundancy

The self-directed MAS exercises generate similar information. They identify interests, values, abilities, and skills you already possess. While aptitude and achievement tests may yield similar information, the self-directed exercises have three major advantages over the standardized tests: less expensive, self-monitored and evaluated, and measure motivation and ability.

Completing each exercise demands a different investment of your time. Writing your life history and completing the Motivated Skills Exercise are the most time consuming. On the other hand, Holland's *Self-Directed Search* can be completed in a few minutes. But the more time you invest with each technique, the more useful information you will generate.

We recommend creating redundancy by using at least two or three different techniques. This will help reinforce and confirm the validity of your observations and interpretations. If you have a great deal of work experience, we recommend using the more thorough exercises. The more you put into these techniques and exercises, the greater the benefit to other stages of your job search. You will be well prepared to target your job search toward specific jobs that fit your MAS as well as communicate your qualifications loud and clear to employers. A carefully planned career or career change should not do less than this.

Bridging Your Past and Future

Many people want to know about their future. If you expect the self-assessment techniques in this chapter to spell out your future, you will be disappointed. Fortune tellers, horoscopes, and various forms of mysticism may be what you need.

We use historical devices which integrate past achievements, abilities, and motivations into a coherent framework for projecting future performance. They clarify past strengths and recurring motivations for targeting future jobs. Abilities and motivations are the qualifications employers expect for particular jobs. Qualifications consist of your past experience and your motivated abilities and skills.

The assessment techniques provide a bridge between your past and future. They treat your future preferences and performance as functions of your past experiences and demonstrated abilities. This common-sense notion is shared by employers: **past performance is the best predictor of future performance**.

Yet, employers hire a person's future rather than their past. And herein lies an important problem you can help employers overcome. Getting the job that is right for you entails communicating to prospective employers that you have the necessary qualifications. Indeed, employers will look for signs of your future productivity for them. You are an unknown and risky quantity. Therefore, you must communicate evidence of your past productivity. This evidence is revealed clearly in your past achievements as outlined in our assessment techniques.

The overall value of using these assessment techniques is that they should enhance your occupational mobility over the long run. The major thrust of all these techniques is to identify abilities and skills which are **transferable** to different work environments. This is particularly important as you change careers. You must overcome employers' negative expectations and objections by clearly communicating your transferable abilities and skills in the most positive terms possible. These assessment techniques are designed to help you do precisely that.

chapter 6

Develop Employer-Centered Objectives

AS a member of the Armed Forces, you are used to setting objectives. However, the objectives you set in the military are normally closely associated with the Commander's mission. Now it's time to formulate objectives based on your desires and goals. What do you want to do? This question will help guide your job search campaign.

Once you identify your interests, skills, and abilities, you should be well prepared to develop a clear and purposeful objective for targeting your job search toward specific organizations and employers. With a renewed sense of direction, and versed in an appropriate language, you should communicate to employers that you are a talented and purposeful individual who achieves results. Your objective must tell employers what you will do for them rather than what you want from them. It targets your accomplishments around employers' needs. In other words, your objective should be employer-centered rather than self-centered.

Goals and Objectives

Goals and objectives are statements of what you want to do in the future. When combined with an assessment of your interests, values, abilities, and skills related to specific jobs, they give your job search needed direction and meaning for the purpose of targeting specific employers. Without them, your job search may flounder as you present an image of uncertainty and confusion to potential employers.

When you identify your strengths, you also create the necessary database and vocabulary for developing your job objective. Using this vocabulary, you should be able to communicate to employers that you are a talented and purposeful individual who achieves results.

If you fail to do the preliminary self-assessment work necessary for developing a clear objective, you will probably wander aimlessly in a highly decentralized, fragmented, and chaotic job market looking for interesting jobs you might fit into. Your goal, instead, should be to find a job or career that is compatible with your interests, motivations, skills, and talents as well as related to a vision of your future. In other words, try to find a job fit for you and your future rather than try to fit into a job that happens to be advertised and for which you think you can qualify.

Orient Yourself to Employers' Needs

Your objective should be a concise statement of what you want to do and what you have to offer to an employer. The position you seek is "what you want to do"; your qualifications are "what you have to offer." Your objective should state your strongest qualifications for meeting the employer's needs. It should communicate what you have to offer an employer without emphasizing what you expect the employer to do for you. In other words, your objective should be work-centered, not self-centered; it should not contain trite phrases which emphasize what you want, such as give me a(n) "opportunity for advancement," "position working with people," "progressive company," or "creative position." Such phrases are viewed as canned job search language which says little of value about you. Above all, your objective should reflect your honesty and integrity; it should not be "hyped."

Your objective is a statement of what you want to do and what you have to offer.

Identifying what it is you want to do can be one of the most difficult job search tasks. Indeed, most job hunters lack clear objectives. Many engage in a random, and somewhat mindless, search for jobs by identifying available job opportunities and then adjusting their skills and objectives to fit specific job openings. While you can get a job using this approach, you may be misplaced and unhappy with what you find. You will fit into a job rather than find a job that is fit for you.

Knowing what you want to do can have numerous benefits. First, you define the job market rather than let it define you. The inherent fragmentation and chaos of the job market should be advantageous for you, because it enables you to systematically organize job opportunities around your specific objectives and skills. Second, you will communicate professionalism to prospective employers. By clearly specifying your interests, qualifications, and purposes, you place yourself ahead of most other applicants. Third, being purposeful means being able to communicate to employers what you want to do. Employers are not interested in hiring indecisive and confused individuals, especially those who do not know what they want to do. Such individuals may become unhappy employees who quit after only a few months on the job. Employers want to know what it is you can do for them. With a clear objective, based upon a thorough understanding of your motivated skills and interests, you can take control of the situation as you demonstrate your value to employers.

Finally, few employers really know what they want in a candidate. Like most job seekers, employers lack clear employment objectives and knowledge about how the job market operates. If you know what you want and can help the employer define his or her "needs" as your objective, you will have achieved a tremendously advantageous position in the job market.

Be Purposeful and Realistic

Your objective should communicate that you are a purposeful individual who achieves results. It can be stated over different time periods as well as at various levels of abstraction and specificity. You can identify short-, intermediate-, and long-range objectives and very general to very specific objectives. Whatever the case, it is best to know your prospective audience before deciding on the type of objective. Your objective should reflect your career interests as well as employers' needs.

Objectives also should be realistic. You may want to become president of the United States or solve all the world's problems. However, these objectives are probably unrealistic. While they may represent your ideals and fantasies, you need to be more realistic in terms of what you can personally accomplish in the immediate future. What, for example, are you prepared to deliver to prospective employers over the next few months? While it is good to set challenging objectives, you can overdo it. Refine your objective by thinking about the next major step or two you would like to make in your career advancement.

Project Yourself Into the Future

Even after identifying your abilities and skills, specifying an objective can be the most difficult and tedious step in the job search process; it can stall the resume writing process indefinitely. This simple one-sentence, 25-word statement can take days or weeks to formulate and clearly define. Yet, it must be specified prior to writing the resume and engaging in other job search steps. An objective gives meaning and direction to all of your other job search activities.

Your objective should be viewed as a function of several influences. Since you want to build upon your strengths and you want to be realistic, your abilities and skills will play a central role in formulating your work objective. At the same time, you do not want your objective to become a function solely of your past accomplishments and skills. You may be very skilled in certain areas, but you may not want to use these skills in the future. As a result, your values and interests filter which skills you will or will not incorporate into your work objective.

Four major steps are involved in developing a work objective. Each step can be implemented in a variety of ways:

STEP 1: Develop or obtain basic data on your functional/transferable skills, which we discussed in Chapter 4.

STEP 2: Acquire corroborating data about yourself from others, tests, and yourself. Use these resources accordingly:

A. From others: Ask three to five individuals whom you know well to evaluate you according to these questions:

- What are my strengths?
- What weak areas might I need to improve?
- What do I need in a job or career to make me satisfied?

Explain to these people that you believe their candid appraisal will help you gain a better understanding of your strengths and weaknesses from the perspectives of others.

B. From vocational tests: Although we prefer self-generated data, vocationally oriented tests can help clarify, confirm, and translate your understanding of yourself into occupational directions. If you decide to use vocational tests, contact a professional career counselor who can administer and interpret the tests. We suggest taking several of the following tests:

- Strong Interest Inventory
- Myers-Briggs Type Indicator

- Edwards Personal Preference Schedule
- Kuder Occupational Interest Survey
- Vocational Interest Inventory
- Career Assessment Inventory
- Temperament and Values Inventory

C. **From yourself:** Numerous alternatives are available for you to practice redundancy. Refer to the exercises in Chapter 4 that assist you in identifying your work values, job frustrations and dissatisfactions, things you love to do, things you enjoy most about work, and your preferred interpersonal environments.

STEP 3: Project your values and preferences into the future by completing simulation and creative thinking exercises:

A. **Ten-Million Dollar Exercise:** First, assume that you are given a $10,000,000 gift; now you don't have to work. Since the gift is restricted to your use only, you cannot give any part of it away. What will you do with your time? At first? Later on? Second, assume that you are given another $10,000,000, but this time you are required to give it all away. What kinds of causes, organizations, charities, etc. would you support?

B. **My Ideal Work Week:** Starting with Monday, place each day of the week at the heading of seven sheets of paper. Develop a daily calendar with 30-minute intervals, beginning at 7am and ending at midnight. Your calendar should consist of a 118-hour week. Next, beginning at 7am on Monday (sheet one), identify the ideal activities you would enjoy doing, or need to do, for each 30-minute segment during the day. Assume you are capable of doing anything; you have no constraints except those you impose on yourself. Furthermore, assume that your work schedule consists of 40 hours per week. How will you fill your time? Be specific.

C. **My Ideal Job Description:** Develop your ideal future job. Be sure you include:

- Specific interests you want to build into your job
- Work responsibilities
- Working conditions
- Earnings and benefits
- Interpersonal environment
- Working circumstances, opportunities, and goals

Write a 2-page description of your ideal job. After completing this exercise, synthesize the job and write a detailed paragraph which describes the kind of job you would most enjoy:

STEP 4: Test your objective against reality. Evaluate and refine it by conducting market research, a force field analysis, library research, and informational interviews.

A. **Market Research:** Four steps are involved in conducting this research:

1. **Products or services:** Based upon all other assessment activities, make a list of 10 things you do or make.

2. **Market:** Identify who needs, wants, or buys what you do or make. Be

specific. Include individuals, groups, and organizations. Then, identify what specific needs your products or services fill. Next, assess the results you achieve with your products or services.

3. **New Markets:** Brainstorm a list of who else needs your products or services. Think about ways of expanding your market. List any new needs your current or new market has which you might be able to fill.

4. **New products and/or services:** List any new products or services you can offer or new needs you can satisfy.

B. Force Field Analysis: Once you have developed a tentative or firm objective, force field analysis can help you understand the various internal and external forces affecting the achievement of your objective. Force field analysis follows a specific sequence of activities:

1. Clearly state your objective or course of action.
2. List the positive and negative forces affecting your objective. Specify the internal and external forces working for and against you in terms of who, what, where, when, and how much. Estimate the impact of each force upon your objective.
3. Analyze the forces. Assess the importance of each force upon your objective and its probable effect upon you. Some forces may be irrelevant to your goal. You may need additional information to make a thorough analysis.
4. Maximize positive forces and minimize negative ones. Identify actions you can take to strengthen positive forces and to neutralize, overcome, or reverse negative forces. Focus on real, important, and probable key forces.
5. Assess the feasibility of attaining your objective and, if necessary, modifying it in light of new information.

C. Conduct Online and Library Research: This research should strengthen and clarify your objective. Consult various reference materials on alternative jobs and careers. Most of these resources are available at your local library or bookstore. Many of the resources traditionally found in libraries are now online. The following websites function as excellent gateways, online databases, and research tools:

- CEO Express — www.ceoexpress.com
- Hoover's Online — www.hoovers.com
- D&B's Million Dollar Database — www.dnbmdd.com/mddi
- Corporate Information — www.corporateinformation.com
- BizTech Network — www.brint.com
- AllBusiness — www.allbusiness.com
- GlassDoor — www.glassdoor.com
- Business.com — www.business.com
- America's Career InfoNet — www.acinet.org
- Newspapers.com — www.newspapers.com
- Salary.com — www.salary.com
- Annual Report Service — www.annualreportservice.com
- Chamber of Commerce — www.chamberofcommerce.com
- Daily Stocks — www.dailystocks.com
- Forbes Lists — www.forbes.com/lists
- Fortune — www.forune.com
- Harris InfoSource — www.harrisinfo.com
- Inc. 5000 — www.inc.com/inc5000

- Moody"s www.moodys.com
- NASDAQ www.nasdaq.com
- Standard & Poors **www.standardandpoors.com**
- ThomasNet® www.thomasnet.com

Directories of Career and Job Alternatives

- *Enhanced Guide for Occupational Exploration*
- *Guide to Occupational Exploration*
- *Occupational Outlook Handbook*
- *Occupational Outlook Quarterly*
- *O*NET Dictionary of Occupational Titles*

Industrial Directories

- *Bernard Klein's Guide to American Directories*
- *Dun and Bradstreet's Middle Market Directory*
- *Dun and Bradstreet's Million Dollar Directory*
- *Encyclopedia of Business Information Sources*
- *Geography Index*
- *Poor's Register of Corporations, Directors, and Executives*
- *Standard Directory of Advertisers*
- *The Standard Periodical Directory*
- *Standard and Poor's Industrial Index*
- *Standard Rate & Data Business Publications Directory*
- *Thomas' Register of American Manufacturers*

Associations

- *Encyclopedia of Associations*
- *National Trade and Professional Associations*
- Access thousands of associations online through the Internet Public Library: www.ipl.org/div/aon

Government Sources

- *The Book of the States*
- *Congressional Directory*
- *Congressional Staff Directory*
- *Congressional Yellow Book*
- *Federal Directory*
- *Federal Yellow Book*
- *Municipal Yearbook*
- *Taylor's Encyclopedia of Government Officials*
- *United Nations Yearbook*
- *United States Government Manual*
- *Washington Information Directory*

Newspapers

- Major city newspapers and trade newspapers. Many are available online through these major gateway sites: www.onlinenewspapers.com and www.newspapers.com.
- Your targeted city newspaper—the Sunday edition.

Business Publications

- *Business Week, Economist, Fast Company, Forbes, Fortune, Harvard Business Review, Newsweek, Red Herring, Smart Money, Time, U.S. News and World Report.* Many of these and other business-oriented publications can be viewed online through www.CEOExpress.com.
- Annual issues of publications surveying the best jobs and employers for the year: *Money, Fortune, Forbes*, and *U.S. News and World Report*. Several of these reports, and publications are available online: http://money.cnn.com, www.fortune.com, and www.forbes.com/lists

Other Library Resources

- Trade journals (refer to the *Directory of Special Libraries and Information Centers* and *Subject Collections: A Guide to Specialized Libraries of Businesses, Governments, and Associations*).
- Publications of Chambers of Commerce; state manufacturing associations; and federal, state, and local government agencies
- Telephone books – The Yellow Pages
- Trade books on "how to get a job"

D. Conduct Informational Interviews: This may be the most useful way to clarify and refine your objective. We'll discuss this procedure in subsequent chapters.

After completing these steps, you will have identified what it is you can do (abilities and skills), enlarged your thinking to include what it is you would like to do (aspirations), and probed the realities of implementing your objective.

Your work objective is a function of both subjective and objective information as well as idealism and realism. We believe the strongest emphasis should be placed on your competencies and should include a broad database. Your work objective is realistic in that it is tempered by your past experiences, accomplishments, skills, and current research. An objective formulated in this manner permits you to think beyond your past experiences.

State a Functional Objective

Your job objective should be oriented toward skills and results or outcomes. You can begin by stating a functional job objective at two different levels: a general objective and a specific one for communicating your qualifications to employers both on resumes and in interviews. Thus, this objective-setting process sets the stage for other key job search activities. For the general objective, begin with the statement:

Stating Your General Objective

I would like a job where I can use my ability to ______, which will result in ______.

SOURCE: Richard Germann and Peter Arnold, *Bernard Haldane Associates Job & Career Building* (New York: Harper and Row, 1980), 54-55.

The objective in this statement is both a *skill* and an *outcome*. For example, you might state:

I would like a job where my experience in program development, supported by innovative decision-making and systems engineering abilities, will result in an expanded clientele and a more profitable organization.

At a second level you may wish to rewrite this objective in order to target it at various consulting firms. For example, on your resume it becomes:

Job-Targeted Objective

An increasingly responsible research position in consulting, where proven decision-making and systems engineering abilities will be used for improving organizational productivity.

The following are examples of weak and strong objective statements:

Weak Objectives

- *Management position which will use business administration degree and will provide opportunities for rapid advancement.*
- *A position in social services which will allow me to work with people.*
- *A position in Personnel Administration with a progressive firm.*
- *Sales Representative with opportunity for advancement.*

Stronger Objectives

- *To use computer science training in software development for designing and implementing operating systems.*
- *A public relations position which will maximize opportunities to develop and implement programs, to organize people and events, and to communicate positive ideas and images.*
- *A position as a General Sales Representative with a pharmaceutical house which will use chemistry background and ability to work on a self-directed basis in managing a marketing territory.*
- *A position in data analysis where skills in mathematics, computer programming, and deductive reasoning will contribute to new systems development.*
- *Responsible position in investment research and analysis. Interests and skills include securities analysis, financial planning, and portfolio management. Long range goal: to become a Certified Financial Planner.*

It is important to relate your objective to your audience. While you definitely want a good job, your audience wants to know what you can do for them. Hence, your objective should be work-centered, not self-centered.

We will return to this discussion when we examine how to develop the objective section on your resume. Your objective will become the key element for organizing all other elements on your resume. It gives meaning and direction to your job search.

chapter 7

Create Dynamite Resumes and Letters

NOW THAT YOU KNOW (1) what you do well, (2) what you enjoy doing, and (3) what you want to do in the future—assuming you have completed the exercises in the four previous chapters—you have the basic information necessary for communicating your qualifications to employers. But what will you do with this information? What messages do you want to send to employers about yourself? How do you plan to convey these messages—by telephone, letter, e-mail, or in face-to-face meetings?

Use Resume Assistance Designed for You

We realize this may be your first resume upon leaving the service. Because it is so important to your job search, your resume needs to be expertly crafted with both your goals and employers' needs in mind. You can obtain assistance through the Transition Assistance Program office and other federally sponsored programs in developing resumes, from mini-resumes appropriate for electronic databases to the traditional one- to two-page resumes appropriate for applications, networking, and job interviews. In Chapter 3 we identified several of these military service, federal government, and association-sponsored transition services available to assist you at no or minimal cost. For example, you can attend resume writing classes available through the auspices of your local TAP office. Transition specialists will review and help you refine your resume at no cost. Some of the military associations we discussed in Chapter 3 will also help you craft your resume albeit for a minimal fee. We recommend that you initially draft the resume on your own using a word processor. By drafting the first version yourself, you will be forced to organize your thoughts in regard to the jobs you've held and your accomplishments in each. In the final analysis, the resume represents you—and who knows you better than yourself? After you've drafted your resume, visit the specialists at your local TAP office or elsewhere and ask for a critique of your efforts. These people have reviewed hundreds of resumes and will be able to expertly evaluate yours. Remember, you are looking for honest feedback rather than a pep talk. These specialists are professionally trained in the art of resume writing. They will ensure your resume effectively communicates your qualifications.

Communicating Positive Images

At every stage in the job search you must communicate a positive image to potential employers. The initial impression you make on an employer through applications, resumes, letters, telephone calls, or informational interviews will determine whether the employer is interested in interviewing you and offering you a position.

Unfortunately, many resumes exhibit these deadly characteristics which are often reported by employers as major weaknesses:

- Unfamiliar military acronyms
- Poor layout
- Misspellings and punctuation errors
- Poor grammar
- Unclear purpose
- Too much military jargon
- Irrelevant data
- Too long or too short
- Poorly typed and reproduced
- Unexplained time gaps
- Too boastful
- Lacks permanent contact information
- Difficult to understand or interpret
- Overstating one's qualifications

Keep in mind that most employers are busy people who normally glance at a resume for only 20 or 30 seconds. Your resume, therefore, must sufficiently catch their attention to pass the 20- to 30-second evaluation test. When writing your resume, ask yourself the same question a hiring manager would ask: "*Why should I read this resume or contact this person for an interview?*" Your answer should result in an attractive, interesting, unique, and skills-based resume.

Writing Resumes

Resumes are important tools for communicating your purpose and capabilities to employers. While many jobs only require a completed application form, you should always prepare a resume for influencing the hiring process. Application forms do not substitute for resumes.

In this chapter, we will look at the various resume formats and provide some rules-of-thumb to help you choose the format most appropriate to your needs. However, regardless of which resume format you select, it must clearly and succinctly convey your qualifications to prospective employers. Before we move on to the details of resume writing, let's take a moment to examine some resume myths.

Many myths surround resumes and other forms of job search correspondence. Some people still believe a resume should summarize one's history. Others believe it will get them a job. And still others believe they should be mailed in response to classified ads. The reality is this: A resume advertises your qualifications to prospective employers. It is your calling card for getting interviews.

Types of Resumes

You have three basic types of resumes to choose from: chronological, functional, and combination. Each format has various advantages and disadvantages, depending on your background and purpose.

The **chronological resume** is the standard resume used by most applicants. It comes in two forms: traditional and improved. The **traditional chronological resume** is also known as the "obituary resume," because it both "kills" your chances of getting a job and is a good source for writing your obituary. Summarizing your work history, this resume lists dates and names first, and duties and responsibilities second; it includes extraneous information such as height, weight, age, marital status, gender, and hobbies. While relatively easy to write, this is the most ineffective resume you can produce. Its purpose at best is to inform people of what you have done in the past as well as where, when, and with whom. It tells employers little or nothing about what you want to do, can do, and will do for them.

The **improved chronological resume** directly communicates your purpose, past achievements, and probable future performance. You should use this type of resume when you have extensive experience directly related to a position you seek. This resume should include a work objective which reflects both your work experience and professional goals. The work experience section should include the names and addresses of former employers followed by a brief description of your accomplishments, skills, and responsibilities; inclusive employment dates should appear at the end. Do not begin with dates; they are the least significant element in the descriptions. Be sure to stress your accomplishments and skills rather than your formal duties and responsibilities. You want to inform your audience that you are a productive and responsible person who gets things done—a doer. Military personnel with a great deal of progressive work experience relevant to the civilian work world should use this type of resume. However, for this resume to work best, you must make sure your military experience has been clearly translated into the language of the civilian work world. It is your responsibility—not the employer's—to translate your military work experience into civilian language.

Functional resumes should be used by individuals making a significant career change, first entering the workforce, or reentering the job market after a lengthy absence. This resume should stress your accomplishments and transferable skills regardless of previous work settings and job titles. This could include responsibilities and accomplishments as a volunteer worker, housewife, or Sunday school teacher. Names of employers and dates of employment should not appear on this resume.

Functional resumes have certain weaknesses. While they are important bridges for the inexperienced and for those making a career change, some employers dislike these resumes. Since many employers still look for names, dates, and direct job experience, this type of resume does not meet their expectations. Use a functional resume only if you have limited work experience or your past work experience does not strengthen your objective when making a major career change.

Combination resumes are a compromise between chronological and functional resumes. Having more advantages than disadvantages, this resume may be exactly what you need as you make a career change with military experience relevant to a civilian career.

Combination resumes have the potential to both meet and raise the expectations of employers. You should stress your accomplishments and skills as well as include your work history. Your work history should appear as a separate section immediately following your presentation of accomplishments and skills in the "Areas of Effectiveness" or "Work Experience" section. It is not necessary to include dates unless they enhance your resume. This is the appropriate resume format for someone with work experience who wishes to change to a job in a related career field.

For most transitioning military, we recommend the combination format because it highlights your functional expertise and also shows your most recent assignments in reverse chronological order. However, many companies, especially defense contractors, want to see a chronological resume because it provides an unbroken chain of work experience, coupled with your levels of responsibility and accomplishments in each job. A small number of readers may choose to select the functional resume format which is most relevant for those seeking employment outside the career field in which they have been working. Examples of these different types of resumes are included later in this chapter.

For further assistance in developing your resume, see our separate resume and letters writing book, *Military-to-Civilian Resumes and Letters* (Impact Publications).

Conventional Versus Electronic Resumes

Employers generally receive resumes in one of three ways—as a paper copy, as an electronic resume (e.g., Microsoft Word, Adobe pdf), or by downloading the candidate's resume from a database. The resume format that you use will depend on the circumstance. For example, if you are going to attend a job fair, you will want to bring paper copies. If, on the other hand, you are surfing the Net and find an opportunity of interest, you will want to send them an electronic resume, most likely in Microsoft Word or Adobe pdf format.

Another form of the electronic resume is the inputting of one's resume via a company's website. Generally this will require you to either upload your resume as a file or "copy and paste" your resume into a standard electronic form and then enter additional pieces of data such as security clearance level, education level, willingness to relocate, etc. In addition to the individual company website, you would be well served to enter your resume into general employment websites such as Monster (www.Monster.com) and Career Builder (www.CareerBuilder.com) and military-specific sites like Corporate Gray Online (www.CorporateGray.com).

In some instances, companies will scan the paper resumes they receive and then store those resumes in their resume database for later retrieval. If so, you will also want to send them an electronic version of your resume.

Constructing Your Resume

Before sitting down to draft your resume, we suggest you collect all the efficiency/performance reports you received while serving in the military. As you read through these reports, think about the responsibilities you held and your accomplishments in each. Now go to the next step. For each assignment, write down on a single sheet of paper (or preferably use a computer—perhaps one at your local TAP office) what you can remember about that assignment. Use your efficiency reports to jog your memory. What was it that you liked? Disliked? Did you hold any leadership positions? If so, how many people reported to you? Did you have a budget and, if so, how much was it? What were the significant skills you developed during that period? What were your important accomplishments? Can you quantify them? What did you do during your off-duty hours? Can you remember any extraordinary event or accomplishment? If so, what was it? Did you do any volunteer work that might show how you reached out to help others? Were you ever stationed overseas? If so, did you learn to speak a foreign language? Are you already bilingual? Did you work on a college or advanced degree?

After documenting your experience and quantifying your accomplishments for each assignment, read through what you have written. Consider how your experience and accomplishments could be stated in a way that civilian readers will understand. What character traits did you exhibit that a prospective hiring manager would find favorable? Again, how can you translate these traits in a succinct, meaningful manner? As for your off-duty activities, is there anything that you did that could be transformed from a hobby into a job—even a part-time job?

Once you've completed this mini-exercise, take out a clean sheet of paper or move to a new page and create a template using the improved chronological resume format. Start with the **Contact Information**—your name, address, and phone, fax, and/or e-mail. Second, under **Objective**, enter your employer-centered job or career objective (see Chapter 6 for a recommended format). Third, after **Qualifications Summary**, either develop a short (5- or 6-line) paragraph or put down a few bulleted items that express your best selling points. Fourth, starting with your most recent assignment and working backwards, enter the different assignments (**Employment History** or **Professional Experience**) you held, along with a brief description of your responsibilities and, more importantly, your accomplishments. Where possible, try to quantify an accomplishment in a way that shows you did something measurably better, faster, or cheaper. Fifth, include relevant **Education and Training**. Finally, if you have **Personal Data** relevant to your objective, put it down. For example, if you want to be a Russian translator and you speak Russian fluently, make sure you include this fact under Personal Data. Be careful in including any other type of information on your resume. Other information most often is extraneous or negative. You should only include information designed to strengthen your stated objective.

You have just created the first draft of your resume. That wasn't too difficult, was it? While your first draft may run more than two pages, try to get everything into one or two pages for the final draft. Most employers lose interest after reading the first two pages.

Your final draft should conform to the following "do's" and "don'ts":

Resume "Do's"

- Do include an employer-centered objective.
- Do focus on those accomplishments that relate to the employers' needs.
- Do use action verbs and the active voice.
- Do include nouns so your resume can be scanned for keywords.
- Do be direct, succinct, and expressive with your language.
- Do appear neat, well organized, and professional.
- Do use ample spacing and highlights (all caps, underlining, bulleting) for different emphases (except if it's an electronic resume).
- Do maintain an eye-pleasing balance. Try to center your contact information at the top, keeping information categories on the left in all caps, and describe the categories in the center and on the right.
- Do check carefully your spelling, grammar, and punctuation.
- Do clearly communicate your purpose and value to employers.
- Do communicate your strongest points first.
- Do seek reviews.
- Do refine, rewrite, and proofread several times.

Resume "Don'ts"

- Don't use military acronyms or slang.
- Don't use abbreviations except for your middle name.
- Don't make the resume cramped and crowded.
- Don't make statements you can't document.
- Don't use the passive voice.
- Don't change the tense of verbs.
- Don't use lengthy sentences and descriptions.
- Don't refer to yourself as "I."
- Don't include negative information.
- Don't include salary information (unless required).
- Don't include a photograph of yourself.
- Don't include extraneous information.

Evaluating the Final Product

You should subject your resume drafts to two types of evaluations. An **internal evaluation** consists of reviewing our lists of "do's" and "don'ts" to make sure your resume conforms to these rules. An **external evaluation** should be conducted by circulating your resume to three or more individuals whom you believe will give you objective and useful feedback. Avoid people who tend to flatter you. The best evaluator would be someone in a hiring position similar to one you will encounter in the actual interview. Ask these people to critique your draft resume and suggest improvements in form and content. Asking someone to critique your resume is one way to spread the word that you are job hunting. As we will see in Chapter 11, this is one method for getting invited to an interview!

Final Production

In today's environment, the norm is to develop your resume on a computer using word processing software and then to print it using a high quality laser printer. (Check with your local TAP office for use of their equipment.)

This approach gives you the flexibility you need to custom design your resume. Use of a laser printer will ensure your resume looks great every time. Always remember, however, to proofread the final copy.

When printing the resume, you must consider the quality and color of paper as well as the number of copies you need. By all means use good quality paper. We recommend watermarked 20-pound or heavier bond paper. Costing 5¢ to 9¢ per sheet, this paper can be purchased through stores like FedEx Office, Staples, and Office Depot. It is important not to cut corners at this point by purchasing cheap paper or using copy machine paper. You might save $10 on 100 copies, but you also will communicate an unprofessional image to employers.

Since we assume you will be using a laser printer, the text color will be black. As for the color of the stationary, we recommend either off-white or a light cream. Your choices of paper quality and color say something about your personality and professional style. Be wise in your selections. If in doubt, ask a career counselor for their opinion.

Whatever choices you make, do not cut costs when it comes to producing your resume. It simply is not worth it. Remember, your resume is your calling card—it should represent your best professional image. Put your best foot forward by producing a first-class resume.

Job Search Letters

Letters also play a key role in a job search. These come in different forms, from cover letters to approach and thank-you letters. Mailed or transmitted letters are normally accompanied by a cover letter. After interviewing for information or a position, you should send a thank-you letter, another type of job search correspondence. Other occasions will arise when it is both proper and necessary for you to write different types of job search letters. Examples of these letters are found in Ron Krannich's *High Impact Resumes and Letters*, *Nail the Cover Letter*, and *201 Dynamite Job Search Letters*.

Your letter writing should follow the principles of good resume and business writing. Job hunting letters are like resumes—they advertise you for interviews. Like good advertisements, these letters should follow four basic principles for effectiveness:

1. Catch the reader's attention.
2. Persuade the reader of your benefit or value.
3. Convince the reader with factual evidence.
4. Move the reader to acquire the product.

Basic Preparation Rules

Before you begin writing a job search letter, ask yourself several questions to clarify the content of your letter:

- What is the purpose of the letter?
- What are the needs of my audience?
- What benefits will my audience gain from me?

- What is a good opening sentence or paragraph for grabbing the attention of my audience?
- How can I maintain the interest of my audience?
- How can I best end the letter so that the audience will be persuaded to contact me?
- If a resume is enclosed, how can my letter best advertise the resume?
- Have I spent enough time revising and proofreading the letter?
- Does the letter represent my best professional effort?

Since your letters are a form of business communication, they should conform to the rules of good business correspondence:

- Plan and organize what you will say by outlining the content of your letter.
- Know your purpose, and structure your letter accordingly.
- Communicate your message in a logical and sequential manner.
- State your purpose immediately in the first sentence and paragraph; main ideas always go first.
- Use short paragraphs and sentences; avoid complex sentences.
- Punctuate properly and use correct grammar and spelling.
- Use simple and straightforward language; avoid jargon.
- Communicate your message as directly and briefly as possible.
- Indicate what follow-up actions you will take.
- End by stating what your reader can expect next from you.

The rules stress how to both organize and communicate your message with impact. At the same time, you should always have a specific purpose in mind as well as know the needs of your audience.

Types of Letters

Cover letters provide cover for your resume. You should avoid overwhelming a one-page resume with a two-page letter or repeating the contents of the resume in the letter. A short and succinct one-page letter which highlights one or two points in your resume is enough. Three paragraphs will suffice. The first paragraph should state your interest and reason for writing. The second paragraph should highlight your possible value to the employer. The third paragraph should state that you will call the individual at a particular time to see if an interview can be scheduled.

Approach letters are written for the purpose of developing job contacts, leads, or information as well as for organizing networks and getting interviews—the subjects of Chapter 10. Your primary purpose should be to get employers to engage in the 5R's of informational interviewing:

- Reveal useful information and advice.
- Refer you to others.
- Read your resume.
- Revise your resume.
- Remember you for future reference.

These letters help you gain access to the hidden job market by making networking contacts that lead to those all-important informational interviews.

Approach letters can be sent out en masse to uncover job leads, or they can target particular individuals or organizations. It is best to target these letters since they have maximum impact when personalized in reference to particular positions.

The structure of approach letters is similar to other letters. The first paragraph states your purpose. In so doing, you may want to use a personal statement for openers, such as "*Mary Tillis recommended that I write to you...*" or "*I am familiar with your...*" State your purpose, but do not suggest that you are asking for a job—only career advice or information. In your final paragraph, request a meeting and indicate you will call to schedule such a meeting at a mutually convenient time.

Thank-you letters, examples of which are included at the end of this chapter, may become your most effective job search letters. They especially communicate your thoughtfulness. These letters come in different forms and are written for various occasions. The most common thank-you letter is written after receiving assistance, such as job search information or a critique of your resume. Other occasions include:

- **Immediately following an interview:** Thank the interviewer for the opportunity to interview for the position. Repeat your interest in the position.
- **Receive a job offer:** Thank the employer for his or her faith in you and express your appreciation.
- **Rejected for a job:** Thank the employer for giving you the "opportunity" to interview for the job. Ask to be remembered for future reference.
- **Terminate employment:** Thank the employer for the experience and ask to be remembered for future reference.
- **Begin a new job:** Thank the employer for giving you this new opportunity and express your confidence in producing the value he or she is expecting from you.

Several of these thank-you letters are unusual, but they all have the same goal in mind—to be remembered by potential employers in a positive light. In a job search, being remembered by employers is the closest thing to being invited to an interview and offered a job. A thank-you letter is a powerful way to get remembered.

Distribution and Management

The only good resumes are those that get read, remembered, referred, and result in a job interview. Therefore, after completing a first-rate resume, you must decide what to do with it. Are you planning to only respond to classified ads with a standard mailing piece consisting of your conventional or electronic resume and a formal cover letter? Do you prefer posting your resume online with resume databases or e-mailing it to potential employers? But wait a minute; classified ads and electronic databases only represent one portion of the job market. What other creative distribution methods might you use, such as sending it to friends, relatives, and former employers? What is the best way to proceed?

Responding to Classified Ads

While most of your writing activities should focus on the hidden job market, at times you may see job listings in newspapers, magazines, and personnel offices to which you would like to respond. While this is largely a numbers game, you can increase your odds by the way you respond to the listings.

You should be selective in your responses. Since you know what you want to do, you will be looking for only certain types of positions. Once you identify them, your response entails little expenditure of time and effort—an envelope, letter, stamp, resume, and maybe 20 minutes of your time. You have little to lose. While you have the potential to gain by sending a cover letter and resume in response to an ad, remember the odds are usually against you.

It is difficult to interpret job listings. Some employers place blind ads with P.O. Box numbers in order to collect resumes for future reference. Others wish to avoid aggressive applicants who telephone or "drop in" for interviews. Many employers work through professional recruiters who place these ads. While you may try to second guess the rationale behind such ads, respond to them as you would to ads with an employer's name, address, or telephone number. Assume there is a real job behind the ad.

Most ads request a copy of your resume. You should respond with a cover letter and resume as soon as you see the ad. Depending on how much information about the position is revealed in the ad, your letter should be tailored to emphasize your qualifications vis-a-vis the ad. Examine the ad carefully. Underline any words or phrases which relate to your qualifications. In your cover letter, you should use similar terminology in emphasizing your qualifications. Keep the letter brief and to the point.

If the ad asks you to state your salary history or salary requirements, state "negotiable" or "open." Alternatively, you can include a figure by stating a salary range 30 to 40 percent above your present military base pay. For example, if your base pay is $30,000 a year, figure your military benefits to be another 25 to 30 percent or $7,500 to $9,000; therefore, your total military compensation, or salary history, at present is closer to $40,000 a year. When you state a salary range, use a figure that is 10 to 20 percent above your total military compensation. Based on your total compensation in the example above, your salary range could be $45,000 to $50,000. If, on the other hand, your base pay is $50,000, add another $10,000 for benefits to arrive at a total compensation figure of $60,000. Your salary requirements could then be in the $67,000 to $72,000 range.

You can increase your odds by the way you respond to job listings.

Use your own judgment in addressing the salary question. There is no hard and fast rule on stating a figure or range. A figure helps the employer screen out individuals with too high a salary expectation. However, most people prefer to keep salary considerations to the end of the interview—after you have demonstrated your value and have more information about the position. We'll return to this question again in Chapter 12 when we address the salary and compensation question.

You may be able to increase your odds by sending a second copy of your letter and resume two or three weeks after your initial response. Most applicants normally reply to an ad during the seven-day period immediately after it appears in print. Since employers often are swamped with responses, your letter and resume may get lost in the crowd. If you send a second copy of your application two or three weeks later, the employer will have more time to give you special attention. By then, he or she also will have a better basis on which to compare you to the others.

Keep in mind that your cover letter and resume may be screened among 400 other resumes and letters. Thus, you want your cover letter to be eye-catching and easy to read. Keep it brief and concise and highlight your qualifications as stated in the employer's ad. Don't spend a great deal of time responding to an ad or waiting anxiously at your mailbox or telephone for a reply. Keep moving on to other job search activities. Your goal should be to contact as many employers as possible because uncovering fruitful job leads is a numbers game.

Self-Initiated Methods

Your letters and resumes can be distributed and managed in various ways. Many people shotgun hundreds of cover letters and resumes to prospective employers. This is a form of gambling where the odds are against you. For every 100 people you contact in this manner, expect one or two who might be interested in you. After all, successful direct-mail experts at best expect only a 2-percent return on their mass mailings!

If you choose to use the shotgun methods, you can increase your odds by using the telephone. Call the prospective employer within a week after he or she receives your letter. Use a carefully prepared telephone script to ensure you say the right words. In so doing, you will probably increase your effectiveness rate from 1 to at least 5 percent.

However, many people are shotgunning their resumes today. As more resumes and letters descend on employers with the increased use of the Internet and online services, the effectiveness rates may be even less.

Your best distribution strategy will be your own modification of the following procedure:

1. Selectively identify for whom you would be interested in working.
2. Send an approach letter.
3. Follow up with a telephone call seeking an appointment for an interview.

It is best not to include a copy of your resume with the approach letter. Keep your resume for the end of the interview. Chapter 10 outlines the procedures for conducting this informational interview.

The Internet

One of the easiest, most cost-effective ways to distribute your resume in today's high-tech environment is through the Internet. While initially a medium for technical positions, its use has expanded, and it is now appropriate for a wide range of positions. It has some obvious advantages. First, it's fast. You can get your resume in the hands of employers in a matter of seconds rather than days through the mail. Second, by providing this information electronically, you are enabling prospective employers worldwide to review your qualifications and match them against your needs. Third, it's free!

Military-Specific Employment Websites

Several resume databases have been organized specifically to facilitate the transition of military personnel into the civilian workforce. Prospective employers electronically access these databases for the purpose of quickly identifying potential job candidates. The principal government site is www.TurboTap.org Sponsored by the U.S. Department of Defense, U.S. Department of Labor, and the U.S. Department of Veterans Affairs, this site is rich with resources appropriate for all service members, including members of the National Guard and Reserve.

Several commercial firms also operate online employment sites designed to link transitioning military with employers. Free to job seekers, the unique Corporate Gray Online (www.CorporateGray.com) site, for example, offers job seekers thousands of employment opportunities with hundreds of military-friendly companies. We also encourage you to visit other military-specific sites where you can post your resume, browse job listings, apply for jobs online, and acquire job search information and advice.

Non-Military Employment Sites

Within the past few years there has been an explosion of online recruitment and job search sites. Indeed, by some estimates there are over 100,000 such sites on the Internet! Most are designed to link employers with job seekers through the use of resume databases and online job postings. Most services are free to job seekers who are encouraged to post their resumes online and browse through thousands of postings. Many of these sites also include useful job search information and advice, from articles to discussion groups and specialized job search services. Our advice: Post your resume to several of the key websites.

So where do you start and which sites are likely to be most useful in your job search? We recommend beginning with several gateway employment sites which provide an overview of the many online resources available to job seekers. Many of these sites will help you decide which sites are best for you. Our favorite gateway sites include:

- Indeed.com www.indeed.com
- AIRS www.airsdirectory.com
- Quintessential Careers www.quintcareers.com
- The Riley Guide www.rileyguide.com
- JobHuntersBible www.jobhuntersbible.com
- Job-Hunt www.job-hunt.org
- Careers.org www.careers.org
- JobSourceNetwork www.jobsourcenetwork.com

The 10 largest employment sites, which are used by thousands of employers and job seekers each day, include:

- Monster.com www.monster.com
- CareerBuilder www.careerbuilder.com
- JobCentral www.jobcentral.com
- CareerOneStop www.jobbankinfo.org
- NationJob www.nationjob.com
- Jobs.com http://jobs.com
- CareerJournal http://online.wsj.com/careers

Other major employment sites well worth visiting include:

- Employment911 www.employment911.com
- EmploymentSpot www.employmentspot.com
- Dice.com www.dice.com
- JobFactory www.jobfactory.com
- Vault.com www.vault.com
- WetFeet.com www.wetfeet.com
- Net-Temps www.net-temps.com
- BestJobsUSA www.bestjobsusa.com
- CareerFlex www.careerflex.com
- SimplyHired.com www.simplyhired.com
- TrueCareers www.truecareers.com
- Job Web www.jobweb.com
- KeneXa http://www.kenexa.com/welcome
- JobBankUSA www.jobbankusa.com
- Employment Guide www.employmentguide.com
- American Preferred Jobs www.preferredjobs.com
- Recruiters Online Network www.recruitersonline.com

In addition to these popular sites, most companies have their own websites which include an employment section encouraging job seekers to apply online for specific positions or enter their resume into the company's resume database. If you are targeting specific companies, be sure to check out their websites for employment information and tips. An excellent example of such a site is the Boston Consulting Group: www.bcg.com.

Record Keeping

Once you begin distributing letters and resumes, you also will need to keep good records for managing your job search writing campaign. Purchase file folders for your correspondence and notes. Be sure to make copies of all letters you write since you may need to refer to them when speaking to employers over the telephone. Record your activities with each employer—letters, resumes, telephone calls, interviews—either in your personal electronic database or set up a card system organized according to the name of the organization or individual. These files will help you quickly access information and evaluate your job search progress.

Always remember the purpose of resumes and letters—*to advertise you for interviews.* They do not get jobs. Since most employers know nothing about you, you must effectively communicate your value in writing prior to the critical interview. While you should not overestimate the importance of this written communication, neither should you underestimate it.

Resume and Letter Examples

The following set of resume and letter examples incorporates many of the writing principles outlined in this chapter as well as relate to the job search strategies specified in other chapters. We provide a mix of chronological and combination resume formats—the formats most relevant to transitioning military personnel. We recommend you use these resumes as a guide. Borrow from whatever resume examples best fit your needs.

Please note that our chronological resume examples stress positions and skills rather than names and dates. We have purposefully de-emphasized work dates by placing them after positions, employers, and locations. Following our previous discussion on placement of resume elements, we always put the most important and eye-catching information first.

Seven sample job search letters designed for different stages of our job search appear the resume examples. Use our examples for tips on developing your own letters. Once you start developing your first two or three letters, we suggest reviewing them with a professional Transition Assistance Program counselor who can give you feedback on the potential effectiveness of your letters. Our goal is to see you through the entire job search process successfully, and crafting effective correspondence is key to your endeavors. Perhaps the most useful advice we could give you at this stage of the process is this: take your time to do it right. Remember to always read and reread your letters. They should represent you at your professional best.

Our examples are not meant to represent military personnel as a whole. Rather, they are presented as instructional devices to assist you in creating your own effective resumes and letters based on a solid understanding of the job search principles outlined in this book. **All of the resumes you find in this book are downloadable as Microsoft Word files on www.CorporateGray.com.** Click the "Post Resumes" link after logging into the site.

Additional resume and cover letter examples appropriate for transitioning servicemembers are found in *Military-to-Civilian Resumes and Letters* (Impact Publications).

Remember, your resume and letters are your personal calling cards. They should convey your qualifications in a manner that catches the reader's attention and quickly illustrates how your skills and experience can be used to a prospective employer's advantage.

For a handy checklist of Resume Do's and Don'ts and to download sample resumes and letters, visit www.CorporateGray.com and click on the Transition Guide tab.

Helicopter Maintenance Supervisor

Available: May 1, 20__

Aurelio Rodriguez

432 Sailors Pointe
San Diego, CA 99212
619-231-3223 RodriguezA@yahoo.com

OBJECTIVE Helicopter Maintenance Supervisor for a company that provides the U.S. Navy with aviation equipment and support.

MILITARY EXPERIENCE

Maintenance Instructor, Naval Base San Diego, 2005-Present

Instructed and graduated 465 students amassing 220 podium hours in 48 classes in Quality Assurance, Work Center Supervisor, and Maintenance Action Form/Subsystem Capability Impact Reporting Organizational Level. Course Curriculum Model Manager of a Chief of Naval Operations approved course in Work Center Supervisor. Achievements:

- Qualified 4 new instructors in Aviation Maintenance Administration Management.
- Successfully piloted 2 new courses – one in organizational maintenance, another in quality assurance.
- Twice nominated for Instructor of the Quarter.

Maintenance Supervisor, Helicopter Anti-Submarine Squadron 2, San Diego, 2001-04

Supervised 5 personnel in performing scheduled and unscheduled maintenance on the SH-60 F/H helicopter. Performed a wide range of maintenance activities affecting the power plants and transmission systems. Achievements:

- Received the highest rating possible from higher headquarters following detailed inspection of assigned helicopters.
- Received promotion based on superior performance ratings.
- Earlier assignments were helicopter maintenance-related and of increasing scope and responsibility during the years 1988 - 2001.

SECURITY CLEARANCE

Top Secret with current Special Background Investigation

EDUCATION

B.S. Aeronautical Engineering, San Diego State University, 2004
3.5 GPA; Dean's List every semester

AWARDS & HONORS

Navy Achievement Medal

Navy Commendation Medal

Law Enforcement Officer

Available: Immediately

703.111.2222 **JOHN T. KING** **kingj@aol.com**

221 King Street
Alexandria, VA 22201
(703) 111-2222

OBJECTIVE: Government law enforcement position where leadership skills and military police experience will benefit a police force seeking dedicated, culturally sensitive, law enforcement professionals.

CAREER SUMMARY: Possess extensive Physical Security and Law Enforcement background, including over 7 years experience in security, police patrolling, supervision, and management. Assertive, take-charge leader ready to apply skills in a corporate setting.

WORK EXPERIENCE

Fort Belvoir, Operations NCO, 437th Military Police Company **2005-Present**

Responsible for managing the daily operations of over 200 Military Police soldiers across a myriad of security-related assignments. Key accomplishments:

- Responded to short-suspense taskings with ease and professionalism. Ensured that the right mix of security professionals were deployed to handle all assigned missions.
- Ensured emergency response actions were properly coordinated with local police and state agencies in a timely manner.
- Coordinated, scheduled, and led unit weapon training and field exercises.

Fort Belvoir, Platoon Sergeant, 437th Military Police Company **2000-2004**

Responsible for the health, welfare, morale, and training of the 32 soldiers in my platoon. Key accomplishments:

- Supervised all daily law enforcement operation.
- Established new suspect apprehension procedures which resulted in a 25% decrease in injuries to law enforcement professionals.
- Implemented computer-based training program that enabled the company to take advantage of "best practice" civilian policing programs.

EDUCATION and TRAINING

A.S. in Administrative Justice, Northern Virginia Community College, Annandale, VA 2004
Diploma, Robert E. Lee High School, Springfield, VA, 1988

Military Police Basic Course, 1988
Drill Sergeant School (Honor Graduate), 1992
Protective Service Course, 1996
Military Police Instructor Training Course, 2003

Available: Immediately

JARROD NOBLE

2525 Second Street, Fayetteville NC // (910) 999-9999 // JarrodNoble@comcast.net

Award winning and highly accomplished Network Administrator with proven track record of reducing operating expenses and increasing productivity.

HIGHLIGHT OF QUALIFICATIONS

- Nine years of experience in network administration & technical troubleshooting.
- Outstanding record of resourceful cost reduction.
- Reputation for exceptional leadership and for consistently performing at the highest level.
- Knowledgeable in wide variety of networking environments and software applications.
- Team player with excellent interpersonal and communication skills.

COMPUTER SKILLS

Operating Systems: Windows NT 4.0 and 3.51, Windows for Workgroups 3.11, WANG COBOL
Software Applications: MS Office 2000, MS Exchange and MS Outlook, MS Internet Explorer
Networking Protocols: TCP/IP, NetBui
Hardware: Personal computers and laptops, backup domain controllers, print servers, HP Laser-jet printers, high speed printers, and related peripherals: DVD/CD ROMs, scanners, modems, etc.

TRANSFERABLE SKILLS AND ACCOMPLISHMENTS

NETWORK ADMINISTRATION

Responsible for all software and hardware utilized by squadron personnel. Key accomplishments:

- Successfully maintained, troubleshot, and repaired array of hardware & software applications.
- Oversaw all user accounts, assigned security rights, and provided desktop support.
- Prepared and coordinated all data file transfers with local and outside agencies.
- Fully accountable for over 400 pieces of computer equipment valued at over $1.5 million.
- Provided PC configuration, procurement and installation.
- Saved over $30,000 as a result of transferring 10 computer systems to support and trouble-shoot system deficiencies.
- Demonstrated solid expertise during 4 infrastructure upgrade projects worth over $200K.
- Oversaw multiple distribution hubs, 6 network servers, and miles of network cable supporting over 200 workstations and network peripherals.
- Dramatically improved computer peripheral inventory by introducing aggressive inspection schedules. Result: 100% item accountability.

MANAGEMENT & TRAINING

Responsible for all training of computer systems, software applications, local and wide area networks, and peripheral equipment. Key accomplishments include:

- Currently manage mainframe and Windows NT computer systems supporting 150 users.
- Supervised and trained over 50 individuals in Mainframe Information Management Systems.
- Saved thousands of dollars by establishing training classroom and revitalizing productivity.
- Exceeded facility's goals by training over 98% of squadron personnel.
- Trained all users and wrote over 100 pages of operating manual.
- Managed all phases of work order completion from receipt of order to finished product.

JARROD NOBLE **Page 2 of 2**

OPERATIONS

Full profit and loss management responsibility for strategic planning, coordinating scheduling, materiel and equipment handling, and labor & materials cost estimating for 400 employee facility.

- Coordinated and scheduled all jobs with customers and craftsmen.
- Successfully handled approximately 1,000 monthly work orders with an on-time completion rate of nearly 100%.
- Oversaw and implemented the facility's Year 2000 (Y2K) preparations. Single-handedly coordinated with 218 facility managers to ensure smooth operations along with quick and effective troubleshooting of potential problems. Result: No incidents reported.
- Strategically located craftsmen throughout the base for immediate Y2K crisis response.

MILITARY ASSIGNMENTS

2005 - Present **15th Civil Engineering Squadron**, Pope AFB, NC
2000 -2004 **514th Civil Engineering Squadron**, Scott AFB, IL

COURSES ATTENDED

Computer Courses: Windows NT, desktop and server
Management Courses: Non Commissioned Officer Management Seminar. Topics: Effective Communication, Time Management, and Employee Motivation & Supervision

SECURITY CLEARANCE

Top Secret with current Special Background Investigation

AWARDS

Received award for outstanding professional skills and technical knowledge as Network Administrator at the 514th Civil Engineering Squadron, Scott AFB, IL

Employer comments:

Sergeant Noble systematically maintained a stellar Information Protection Program enabling the unit to secure 100% electronic data integrity while maintaining an extremely high level of customer awareness. His wealth of knowledge proved critical during the 123rd Air Support Group's successful transition from the Wang Information Management System to a newer, Year 2000 compatible system. He enforced an automated anti-virus protection program, blanketing 300 computer systems

Citation that accompanied award of the Air Force Commendation Medal.

** Resume provided by Rita Fisher, CPRW; email: RitaFisher33@comcast.net*

Maintenance Technician

Available: Immediately

ELAINE WILLIAMS

34 Sullivan Avenue (703) 999-9999
Fairfax, VA 22313 ewilliams@comcast.net

MAINTENANCE TECHNICIAN

Over 10 years of experience in the maintenance, repair, troubleshooting and operation of highly complex electronics equipment. Technical skills include hydraulic, pneumatic, mechanical, electrical, and electronic systems. Demonstrated ability to train and lead others to perform productively. Comfortable in fast-paced, high-stress environments requiring attention to detail., ability to meet deadlines and quick adaptation to constantly changing priorities.

ACCOMPLISHMENTS

- Completed and achieved the highest number of technical qualifications out of 22 people.
- Selected by senior management as Employee of the Quarter twice in the last year for "superior performance, dedication, professionalism, and positive attitude."
- Recognized as a team player who requires minimum supervision, is motivated to the highest performance standards, and committed to excellence.
- Displayed "unequaled troubleshooting skills in maintenance activities," resulting in the flawless execution of 50+ critical maintenance actions for the safe launch of 10,000+ aircraft.

EMPLOYMENT HISTORY

UNITED STATES NAVY **2005 to Present**

Aircraft Maintenance Technician

Advanced through increasingly responsible positions in aviation equipment operation, maintenance, quality assurance, and safety. Selected by supervisor out of 22 technicians to handle one of the most complex assignments in the entire division.

Equipment Maintenance & Repair

- Experienced in the operation and maintenance of multi-million dollar aircraft.
- Performed troubleshooting of electrical, hydraulic, pneumatic, and mechanical systems.

Quality Assurance & Inspection

- Accurately calibrated and installed 70+ precision measurement tools valued at over $250K.
- Supervised all maintenance checks to monitor accuracy and adherence to exact procedures.

Training & Team Leadership

- Trained and oversaw 40-member work center in the operation & maintenance of equipment.
- Advanced skills of new personnel, contributing to 15,000+ hours of safe aircraft operations.

EDUCATIONAL TRAINING

Successfully completed specialized training programs in Maintenance Equipment & Operations, Aircraft Firefighting, Catapult Hydraulics, Arresting Gear Hydraulics, and Quality Assurance.

Resume provided by Louise Garver; Louise@careerdirectionsllc.com

Human Resources Manager

Available: March 1, 20__

834 Market Lane
Madison, CT 02521
H: (233) 245-6789 / W: (233) 123-4567
dphillips@aol.com

DANA PHILLIPS

OBJECTIVE

Human Resources position where military recruiting and leadership experience can be used to enhance the operational effectiveness of a company's HR operations.

QUALIFICATIONS

Skilled communicator with proven personnel administration expertise. Unique blend of managerial and hands-on experience acquired over a career with the U.S. Coast Guard. Knowledgeable in all facets of HR management, including staffing, recruiting and retention, benefits, training, and legal issues. Proficient in Spanish. Possess Secret clearance.

AREAS OF EXPERTISE

Personnel Management

- Planned, organized, and managed daily activities of a Human Resources department charged with managing the staffing requirements and availability of sea-based enlisted Coast Guard billets. Used computer models to determine the proper accession numbers, advancement opportunities, and year-end strength goals. Acknowledged by peers and associates for raising the efficiency of the department's personnel management operations. Received Commander's Award for outstanding service.

Administration

- Responsible for the daily administration of personnel administration activities, such as the creation of orders for Coast Guard personnel moving to new duty locations or transitioning from the service. Processed special personnel actions, including awards, promotion orders, disciplinary paperwork, and marriage applications. Ensured all paperwork was completed accurately and within time schedules.

Recruiting

- Served as a front-line human resources recruiter for the U.S. Coast Guard. Interviewed, assessed, and recruited candidates interested in military service. Recognized for consistently exceeding recruitment goals for quantity and quality over a 24-month period. Received Meritorious Service Medal from the East Coast Human Resources Manager.

EMPLOYMENT HISTORY

Human Resource Manager: The Pentagon, Washington, DC, 2005-Present
Branch Chief: Enlisted Military Affairs, Washington, DC, 2002-2004
Detailer: Coast Guard Assignment Branch, Washington, DC, 1999-2001
Seaman: U.S. Coast Guard, 1989-1998

EDUCATION

Associate of Arts, Marine Science, University of Maryland, 2005

Logistics Manager

Available: May 1, 20__

Stephen Jackson

8610 Meredith Court Springfield, VA 22000 703-666-2231 (C) / 703-555-1234 (W) sjackson@earthlink.net

OBJECTIVE: Position as **Logistics Manager** for a company that can use my aviation logistics experience to increase the efficiency and safety of its maintenance operations.

EDUCATION: B.S. Aeronautical Engineering, U.S. Naval Academy, 1992
M.S. Aeronautical Engineering, Naval Post Graduate School, 2004

CAREER SUMMARY:

Extensive experience in aviation maintenance. Strong operational management background. Expertise in the logistical support of a diverse range of aircraft, including tactical military jets and cargo aircraft. Adept problem solver. Skilled and effective manager who led support staff to new levels of excellence in aviation system safety and operational testing.

CORE COMPETENCIES:

Aviation Logistics

Led the maintenance operations for a tactical Marine fighter wing. Responsible for the operational readiness of 135 high performance combat aircraft. Managed the activities of a staff in excess of 200 personnel.

Results: Improved the overall readiness rate from 94.6% to 98.5% by implementing and enforcing strict quality control procedures.

Quality Assurance

Managed a division of 34 maintenance personnel responsible for assuring quality maintenance of 89 F/A-18 aircraft and over $70 million of munitions and ground equipment. Focal point for safety, product improvement and reliability of military aircraft. Administered a $12 million annual budget.

Results: Received an overall maintenance program rating of outstanding. Recognized for innovative problem solving in several complex areas affecting aircraft engine performance.

Safety As the Director of Safety, ensured that maintenance activities were done correctly and in accordance with the appropriate military standards. Continuously checked the maintenance status by conducting both periodic and unannounced inspections of the aircraft. Conserved resources and personnel labor costs through the predictive analysis of aircraft accident reports. Identified problems and initiated actions to correct deficient aircraft systems, operating procedures, and technical data collection.

Results: Reduced the EA-6B fleet-wide accident rate to zero for the first time in its history. Spear- headed effort that solved serious thrust deficien-

STEPHEN JACKSON **Page 2 of 2**

cies. Made proposals for improving saving and reliability by 27%.

Training Developed a flying syllabus that is used to train over 150 crews annually. Authored a Tactical Formation Manual that filled a longstanding void. **Result:** Realized $150,000 cost savings through reduced qualification training time.

EMPLOYMENT HISTORY:

Senior Logistics Officer, U.S. Marine Corps, MCAS El Toro, CA, 2008-present

Director of Safety, U.S. Marine Corps, MCAS Cherry Point, NC, 2007

Training Officer, U.S. Marine Corps, U.S.S. Ranger, 2006

Naval Post Graduate School, Monterey, CA, 2005

Navigator, U.S. Marine Corps, MCAS, El Toro, CA 2003-2004

Junior Officer leadership assignments, U.S. Marine Corps, 2002-2003

SECURITY CLEARANCE: Top Secret (TS-SCI) w/ current Background Investigation

AFFILIATIONS: U.S. Naval Academy Alumni Association, Military Officers Association of America, Boy Scout Leader

Homeland Security Manager

Available: March 1, 20___

David Brown

3211 Guadalcanal Way
San Diego, CA 92111
(619) 222-3333 / BrownD@hotmail.com

OBJECTIVE: A senior-level management position where my skills and military experience can be used to enhance the nation's security.

SUMMARY OF QUALIFICATIONS

As a senior-level Marine Corps officer, have been responsible for a wide range of security and anti-terrorism related activities. In this capacity, have designed and implemented a comprehensive protection scheme to ensure key Government leaders can continue to perform their responsibilities, even under the highest threat levels. Demonstrated ability to complete complex and dangerous missions while remaining sensitive to the morale and well being of those under my charge. Possess a current Top Secret clearance with full life-style polygraph.

CORE COMPETENCIES

- Management
- Team Building
- Leadership
- Problem Solving
- Strategic Planning
- Financial Management

ACCOMPLISHMENTS

Management/Leadership:

Over 20 years of experience training, managing, supervising, and leading diverse organizations to meet warfighting and readiness requirements. Established and led the Fleet-Antiterrorism Security Team Company, the first Marine Corps anti-terrorism unit on the West Coast. Results: High-level awards for the organization's outstanding performance.

Team Building/Problem Solving:

- Developed and orchestrated the reorganization of a 5,000-person organization to more effectively accomplish its mission. Result: Reorganization was completed 90 days in advance of timeline with minimum personnel turbulence and frustration.
- Commanded Marine Corps infantry units at every level up to Brigade. Gained combat experience as a team leader and squad leader in Vietnam. Result: Awarded Navy Achievement Medal with Combat "v" for valor.

DAVID BROWN **Page 2 of 2**

Financial Management:

Developed and supervised the programming, budgeting, and execution of a $150 million operational budget, while achieving cost avoidance of over $10 million in the Marine Corps Recruiting Command. Over 20 years of fiscal management in key leadership billets. Budgets have ranged from $3 million to $150 million.

Strategic Planning:

- Developed, reviewed, and assessed major operational plans for Bosnia and Kosovo while serving on the Joint Staff.
- As Chief of Staff for the Marine Corps Recruiting Command, developed and orchestrated a strategic plan that resulted in major fiscal and personnel efficiencies, including an annual savings of over $67,000.

WORK HISTORY

Chief of Staff, Marine Corps Recruiting Command Quantico, VA, 2007-Present
Orchestrate the development of all aspects of policy, marketing, advertising, sales, facilities, fiscal and personnel management, safety and training of a 5,000-person, civilian and military, organization. Results: Annually recruited 41,000 high quality new men and women, nationwide, with the most successful year in history in FY02. Annual operating budget is $150 million.

Commanding Officer, 3rd Marine Regiment 3rd Marine Division, Hawaii, 2005-2006
Led a 4,000-person crisis force focused on assessing requirements and developing anti-terrorism programs for the Asia-Pacific Region. Maintained a 6-hour crisis response element 365 days per year. Developed major operational plans for strategic events with other countries in the Region. Served as the Marine Corps' Regional Force Commander, overseeing complex planning and execution of maritime forces prepared to respond to security threats throughout the world.

Head, Bosnia Desk, Central Eastern European Division Joint Staff, 2002-2004
Developed strategy, policy and plans for Bosnia security, anti-terrorism operations incident to interactions with senior executive members of the White House, State Department, CIA, NATO, Office of Secretary of Defense, and key European, Russian, and Japanese representatives.

Commanding Officer, 1st Battalion, 3rd Marines, Hawaii 2001-2002
Led a 1,000-person crisis force focused on security, anti-terrorism requirements in the Asia-Pacific Region. Developed anti-terrorism programs. Established training, unit cohesiveness, sound fiscal and personnel management of a short notice reaction force.

EDUCATION

B.S. Degree, Military History, Villanova University, 1988
M.S. Degree, Management Science, Harvard University, 2000

Engineer

Available: June 1, 20___

CHRIS P. JACOBS

*123 Oak Street, Annapolis, MD 21401 * h 410-555-1234 * c 410-666-1234 * cpjacobs@aol.com*

SUMMARY

- Six years Active Duty U.S. Army -- Sergeant E-5 Team Leader
- Strong leadership qualities; takes charge and manages projects to completion
- Creative and resourceful in generating new ideas and solving complex problems.
- Takes initiative. Motivates others to perform at highest levels. Leads by example.
- Background and experience in construction & demolition - military certified.
- Secret security clearance

Quote from recent Army Performance Evaluation

"Outstanding leader; able to accomplish any mission. Possesses the moral courage to do the right thing at all times. Places unit's mission and welfare of his soldiers above personal needs."

SKILLS & EXPERIENCE

SUPERVISORY / LEADERSHIP

- Immediately promoted upon passing the rigorous Sergeant's Board evaluation process.
- Directly supervised, trained, and mentored 10 soldiers
- Led team on over 200 combat patrols earning the respect and loyalty of fellow soldiers.
- Maintained direct accountability for more than $300,000 in military supplies and equipment.

COMMUNICATION / TRAINING

- Conducted 15 classes for the 3rd Brigade Combat Team on military weapons training.
- Provided concise briefings to unit regarding mission, tasks, and objectives.
- Cross-trained personnel as a means of enhancing security and emergency readiness.

WORK HISTORY

Fort Carson, CO	Combat Engineer, Team Leader	June 2008 - Present
Fort Leonardwood, MO	Combat Engineer, Member of Squad	July 2004-2007

EDUCATION

Denver Community College, Denver, CO -- 25 Credit Hours, Construction Management
Diploma, Kendall High School, Jacksonville, FL, 2006

AWARDS & HONORS

Army Commendation Medal, Presidential Unit Citation, National Defense Service Medal

Resume provided by Beth Colley; resume@chesres.com

Electrician

Available: July 1, 20___

FRANCIS X. SEABEE

456 Bay Bridge Lane
San Diego, CA 92111

(619) 555-9999
SeabeeF@aol.com

OBJECTIVE *Position as an electrician for a company that seeks an experienced, skilled technician.*

QUALIFICATIONS

- 6 Years experience as an Industrial Electrician
- Rated superior in technical repair activities
- Demonstrated ability to maintain, operate, repair, and install a wide variety of commercial and industrial electronic equipment

SKILLS SUMMARY

Experienced in preventative and corrective electrical maintenance on the following equipment:

- 3 phase and single phase AC/DC plant equipment
- Power and lighting circuits, switches, and fuse boxes
- Amp meters, volt meters, ohm meters, and other test equipment
- Motors, controllers, and related power generation equipment
- Alarm systems and other power monitoring equipment

Knowledgeable at using the following tools and equipment to troubleshoot and repair equipment malfunctions:

- Logic test equipment
- Power presses
- Automatic-testing
- Undercutting machines
- Spot welding machine
- Coil winding machine
- Trickle and impregnation machine
- Soldering tools

Experienced in reading blueprints/drawings and using the following tools to install or repair cables, conduit, and circuits:

- Conduit benders
- Hand and power tools
- Pipe threaders
- Cable pullers
- Wire and cable cutters

Supervised the operation of turbine generators and emergency diesel generators. Trained junior personnel.

EMPLOYMENT AND TRAINING

Electrician 400 Hz Motor-Generator Maintenance, 2008
Electrician "C" School, 2004
Electrician "A" School, 2003

EDUCATION

Diploma, Edison High School, Edison, NJ, 2004
Certificate (Honor Graduate), AH-64A Armament/ Electrical System Repairer Course, Ft Eustis, VA, 2002

Sales Trainer

Available: June 20- -

JAMES L. PARK

2829 Creekview Court
Quantico, VA 22312
W: (703) 222-3333 / H: (703) 444-5555
ParkJ@aol.com

OBJECTIVE Sales training position for a consumer products company seeking highly motivated individual with oustanding salesmanship skills.

QUALIFICATIONS SUMMARY

RECRUITING

- Interacted with candidates and their parents on a daily basis. Highlighted the benefits of military service.
- Surpassed recruitment goals by 15% annually.
- Visited over 100 local high schools and community colleges to attract top-notch Marine candidates.

TRAINING

- Indoctrinated 150 new recruits in the traditions and practices of the Marine Corps.
- Physically and mentally challenged new recruits, preparing them for a wide range of national security-related assignments.
- Trained new recruits on the use of various weapon systems. Achieved 95% unit proficiency.

MANAGEMENT

- Led and directed the activities of a 10-member team; improved both their individual and team skills.
- Counseled and mentored subordinates, evaluated their performance, and provided developmental advice.

EMPLOYMENT HISTORY

Recruiter, U.S. Marine Corps, Atlanta, GA, 2008-Present

Drill Instructor, U.S. Marine Corps, Paris Island, SC, 2004-2007

Squad Leader, U.S. Marine Corps, Okinawa, Japan, 2002-2003

Member of Squad, U.S. Marine Corps, Okinawa, Japan, 1998-2002

EDUCATION & TRAINING

A.S. Business Administration, Albany Community College, GA, 2009

U.S. Marine Corps Recruiters School, 2008

Advanced Leadership Training, 2001

U.S. Marine Corps Basic Training, 1998

COVER LETTER

2842 South Plaza
Chicago, Illinois 60228
March 12, 20___

David C. Johnson
Director of Personnel
Bank of Chicago
490 Michigan Avenue
Chicago, Illinois 60222

Dear Mr. Johnson:

The accompanying resumé is in response to your listing in the Chicago Tribune for a security officer.

I am especially interested in this position because my experience as a Master-at-Arms has prepared me for understanding the need for a disciplined, secure work environment and the problems associated with unexpected events. I wish to use this experience to protect a growing and community-conscious bank such as yours.

I would appreciate an opportunity to meet with you to discuss how my experience will best meet your needs. My ideas on how to improve your bank's security posture may be of particular interest to you. Therefore, I will call your office on the morning of March 17 to inquire if a meeting can be scheduled at a convenient time.

I look forward to meeting you.

Sincerely yours,

James Peterson

James Peterson

APPROACH LETTER
Referral

821 Stevens Point
Boston, MA 01990
April 14, 20_____

Terri Fulton
Director of Personnel
TRS Corporation
6311 W. Dover
Boston, MA 01991

Dear Ms. Fulton:

Alice O'Brien suggested that I contact you about my interest in personnel management. She said you are one of the best people to talk to in regard to careers in personnel.

I am leaving the U.S. Army after seven years of experience in personnel administration. Because of my positive Army experience, I would like to continue working in a large organization. However, before I venture further into the civilian job market, I would like to benefit from the experience and knowledge of other professionals in the field who might advise me on opportunities for someone with my qualifications.

Perhaps we could meet briefly sometime during the next two weeks to discuss my career plans. I have several questions which I believe you could help clarify. I will call your office on Tuesday, April 22, to schedule a meeting time.

I look forward to discussing my plans with you.

Sincerely yours,

Kristine Kellerman

Kristine Kellerman

THANK YOU LETTER
Post-Informational Interview

9910 Thompson Drive
Cleveland, Ohio 43382
June 21, 20____

Jane Evans, Director
Evans Finance Corporation
2122 Forman Street
Cleveland, Ohio 43380

Dear Ms. Evans:

Your advice was most helpful in clarifying my questions on careers in finance. I am now reworking my resume and have included many of your thoughtful suggestions. I will send you a copy next week.

Thanks so much for taking time from your busy schedule to see me. I will keep in contact and follow through on your suggestion to see Sarah Cook about opportunities with the Cleveland-Akron Finance Company.

Sincerely yours,

Daryl Haines

THANK YOU LETTER
Post-Job Interview

2962 Forrest Drive
Denver, Colorado 82171
May 28, 20_____

Thomas F. Harris
Director, Personnel Department
Coastal Products Incorporated
7229 Lakewood Drive
Denver, Colorado 82170

Dear Mr. Harris:

Thank you again for the opportunity to interview for the marketing position. I appreciated your hospitality and enjoyed meeting you and members of your staff.

The interview convinced me of how compatible my background, interest, and skills are with the goals of Coastal Products Incorporated. As I mentioned during our conversation, my experience as a military recruiter has prepared me well for direct sales opportunities both in the U.S. and Germany. I am confident my work for you will result in increased profits within the first two years.

For more information on my success as a recruiter, please call Commander Dave Garrett at 202/726-0132. I talked to Dave this morning and mentioned your interest in this program.

I look forward to seeing you again.

Sincerely,

Thomas Potman

Thomas Potman

THANK YOU LETTER
Job Offer Acceptance

564 Court Street
St. Louis, MO 53167
April 29, 20___

Mr. Ralph Ullman
President
S.T. Ayer Corporation
6921 Southern Blvd.
St. Louis, MO 53163

Dear Mr. Ullman:

I appreciated your consideration for the Research Associate position. While I am disappointed in not being selected, I learned a great deal about your corporation, and I enjoyed meeting with you and your staff. I felt particularly good about the professional manner in which you conducted the interview.

Please keep me in mind for future consideration. I have a strong interest in your company and believe we would work well together. I will be closely following the progress of your company over the coming months. Perhaps we will be in touch at some later date.

Best wishes.

Sincerely,

Martin Tollins

Martin Tollins

THANK YOU LETTER
Job Offer Acceptance

7694 James Court
San Francisco, CA 94826
June 7, 20____

Ms. Judith Greene
Vice President
Southwest Airlines
2400 Van Ness
Dallas, TX 94829

Dear Ms. Greene:

I am pleased to accept your offer, and I am looking forward to joining you and your staff next month.

The customer relations position is ideally suited to my background and interests. I assure you I will give you my best effort in making this an effective position within your company.

I understand I will begin work on July 7, 20____. If, in the meantime, I need to complete any paperwork or take care of any other matters, please contact me at (303) 777-1234.

I enjoyed meeting with you and your staff and appreciated the professional manner in which the hiring was conducted.

Sincerely,

Joan Kilmer

Joan Kilmer

chapter 8

Secure Federal Employment

GOVERNMENT IS THE SINGLE LARGEST EMPLOYER in the United States. Supporting more than 20 million employees, federal, state, and local government agencies offer numerous attractive opportunities for transitioning servicemembers. Federal government agencies, which employ 2.4 million civilian workers (over 600,000 of these are post office workers), are of special interest to individuals with military backgrounds. Indeed, many veterans look for employment within agencies of the Departments of Defense, Veterans Affairs, and Homeland Security—agencies involved with national security issues of considerable importance to our country. In this chapter, we will identify various resources for finding government employment, discuss the types of government jobs available, explain the job application and selection process, and highlight various military-specific issues of relevance to government employment. While the focus is on federal employment, we address state and local employment at the end of this chapter.

Advantages of Government Service

Working in the public sector has many important advantages . . .

First, as someone who has served in the military, you already have first-hand experience working for the federal government. You know the government culture and how the government operates. In many cases, there is a direct correlation between the work you performed in the armed forces and the types of positions the government is looking to fill today. In fact, there have been many instances when a servicemember took off his or her uniform one day and came back into that same position, but as a civilian, the very next day! And as you will read shortly, the government gives military veterans preference when applying for federal employment.

Second, government salaries are relatively good compared to similar positions in the private sector. This compensation includes excellent health care benefits and a generous pension plan. Important to those who have separated short of military retirement, your time in service can count towards federal employment. Because the rules in this regard can be complex, we encourage you to talk with a government employment specialist.

Third, federal employment tends to be more secure than private sector employment as measured by the relatively low attrition rate from government employment compared to attrition in the private sector.

Fourth, while working conditions vary among the federal agencies, these are generally good. Most federal employees are satisfied with their job, finding it interesting and rewarding. The typical government employee works an 8-hour day, 40-hour week, though this can vary depending on the agency and its mission.

Fifth, when considering employment opportunities in the federal, state, and local government, you will find a wide range of openings across the country and in the U.S. territories.

Sixth, career progression within the federal government is merit based, resulting in general fairness in promotions and advancement. And as a military veteran, your knowledge of the government culture and what it takes to be a top performer, gives you a leg up. In fact, many of the government's star employees used to wear a military uniform.

We're hopeful that your dedication to mission, ability to work in a team environment, and "can do" attitude will enable you to join that distinguished group!

Since there are many benefits to government employment, we encourage you to give it serious consideration. While the federal application process is lengthy (sometimes taking 6 to 8 months), you'll likely find the wait well worth it. If your financial situation requires an income stream while waiting for the federal hiring process to be completed, you might consider temporary or part-time employment. Staffing agencies such as Robert Half International, Adecco, and Manpower are good companies to contact in that regard.

Finding the Job

There are numerous resources available to help you find government jobs, the main one being www.usajobs.gov. All federal agencies are required to post their jobs and this website is often the one selected for that purpose. You can search by series, agency, location, title, and keywords. This site also has a comprehensive Frequently Asked Questions (FAQ) section. You can post your resume here without sending it. The key is to follow the instructions as to what type of resume is acceptable and in what format.

In addition to www.usajobs.gov, many of the military services and agencies run their own websites. For example, job openings within the Department of the Navy can be found at http://federalgovernmentjobs.us/job-agency/department-of-the-navy.html. The Department of the Army's civilian job openings can be found at http://www.cpol.army.mil. And the Air Force's civilian job openings are at https://ww2.afpc.randolph.af.mil/Resweb.

There are also several excellent commercial websites that list government jobs, including the Federal Research Service (www.FedJobs.com), Federal Job Search (www.FederalJobSearch.com), and Federal Jobs Digest (www.jobsfed.com). Most of these organizations also offer fee-based federal job search assistance, as does the Resume Place www.resume-place.com.

In addition to the above resources, you are also encouraged to talk with friends and associates who are working for the government to learn about job opportunities. And you should be aware that the Human Resources departments of all the federal agencies have hardcopies of the federal job announcements available to job seekers.

Understanding Federal Jobs

Each federal job announcement includes the following:

* *Job Title*

* *Series*

Jobs in the federal government are generally defined by a 3- or 4- digit "series" number, similar to a Military Occupational Specialty code or rating. For a list of all the series numbers and job titles, visit www.opm.gov/qualifications.

* *Grade*

The grade relates directly to the salary for the position.

* *Area of Consideration.*

This dictates who is *eligible* to apply for the position. If the Area of Consideration is "all sources" or "status and non-status candidates," that means everyone can apply. If, on the other hand, the Area of Consideration is "status candidates only," that means only current or reinstatement eligible federal employees can apply. However, you may still be eligible to apply for the "status only" positions because of your military service. This exception falls under the Veterans Employment Opportunity Act (VEOA) and will be specifically mentioned in the announcement if it applies to the position.

* *Location*

* *Duties of the Position*

* *Specialized Experience*

* *KSAs (Knowledge, Skills, & Abilities),* sometimes listed as Evaluation Criteria.

* *Application Details*

Provides specifics on how and where to submit your job application.

* *Closing Date*

Date the government hiring office will stop accepting applications for the job.

Competitive vs. Excepted Service

A federal agency can either offer their positions on a competitive basis or on an excepted service basis. If the former, the Office of Personnel Management's Human Resources office manages the hiring process. Excepted agencies, on the other hand, do their own hiring. In this case, they would list the job opening on their website and all interested job seekers would apply directly to that agency, which can hire at any step in the announced pay grade. The excepted agency may also have different pay bands than General Schedule (GS).

Applying for the Position

The first step is to carefully review the job announcement. Are you eligible to apply? Are you comfortable with the duties and where the job is located? Do you have the specialized experience and KSAs the government agency is seeking? Can you submit your application before the closing date? Assuming the answer to these questions is in the affirmative, now it's time to write your federal resume. Before doing so, read OF 510, a brochure titled *Applying for a Federal Job*, for guidance. Some agencies may require the use of OF 612 (*Optional Application for Federal Employment*). These forms are available at www.opm.gov/forms.

The federal resume, unlike the corporate resume, should be long (four to five pages is average) and detailed. To create your resume, you can use the Resume Builder application found in www.usajobs.gov or word processing software such as Microsoft Word. You must tailor your resume to the duties of the position and explain how your experience meets the specialized experience required. You must show that you are qualified for the job at the level required. If you use military acronyms, be sure to explain them. And unlike on a commercial resume, you *do* want to include your Social Security Number (SSN), nationality, and country of citizenship. If you attended senior military schools, include them on your resume. You should put your name, SSN, and job announcement number on every page.

The KSAs (Knowledge, Skills & Abilities) are the most important part of the federal job application process and are normally listed under the heading "Evaluation Criteria." Think of the KSAs as interview questions, and cite examples from your work experience to match each. Your responses can be either in single-spaced narrative or bullet format. The average length of a KSA varies from a page to one-and-a-half pages. The experience required through the KSAs is the minimum experience to be judged qualified. If you can respond affirmatively to 80% of the questions, then go ahead and apply, as that might be good enough depending on the competition.

Your completed job application package should consist of 1) a cover letter (optional), 2) your resume, 3) the KSAs with your responses to each, and 4) any additional information or optional forms that are specified in the job announcement. If you do elect to include a cover letter, make sure to carefully read the announcement so that you include whatever they requested be in that letter, which also sometimes serves as the resume. If any additional or optional forms are required, visit www.opm.gov/forms/html/sf.asp.

Veterans Preference - If at the pay grade of O-3 or below, 5 points are added to a qualified veteran's rating score if s/he served honorably during the Gulf War or from 9/11/2001 to the close of Operation Iraqi Freedom. A veteran leaving with a service-connected disability will receive 10 points. If requesting veterans preference, you must include your DD Form 214. For more information on veterans preference, see www.fedshirevets.gov.

Veteran's Recruitment Appointment (VRA). The government hiring authority can name select you - if you are qualified - up to the GS-11 level. The VRA applies to all active duty military but not to those who have been out of the military for more than two years.

Common mistakes in the job application process include leaving required fields blank, not marking VRA/VEOA (Veterans Employment Opportunity Act), not using the allotted number of characters per experience block, and not following directions. As in active duty in the military, attention to detail is important!

The Selection Process

The government hiring agency will review your job application for completeness and basic qualification. Your application resume will be compared against the KSAs, and a score and numerical ranking will be rendered. Only the top three applicants for the position will be referred for an interview by the hiring manager, who will make the final decision. If you are selected, you will receive an interim offer letter contingent on a background/security check.

The newly hired federal employee is on probation for one year. It takes three years to gain Career Status. Their pay typically starts at Step 1 in the grade hired. For certain hard-to-fill jobs or for applicants with superior qualifications, federal agencies have more latitude with salary. Before being eligible to be promoted to the next level, you need to spend one year at your current level. The federal government recently implemented pay bands and has implemented a "pay-for-performance" program at certain agencies, though this program has generated considerable controversy and is under review.

State and Local Government Employment

Most government jobs are found at the state and local levels. Nearly 17 million individuals work for nearly 87,500 state and local government units. This includes 3,000 counties, 19,500 municipal governments, 16,500 townships, 13,500 school districts, and 35,100 special districts. The state of Illinois has the largest number of government units—6,900—an extreme example of overlapping jurisdictions. Hawaii has the least number of government units—20. The most numerous state and local government employers are found in education (universities and school districts) and criminal justice (police departments and court systems).

You may be interested in exploring these two military transition programs, which are primarily aimed at employment at the state and local levels:

Troops to Teachers – www.ProudToServeAgain.com
Troops to Cops – www.cops.usdoj.gov

The best approach to finding employment with state and local government agencies is to target particular units of government. Each has their own hiring requirements, which usually involve submitting applications and/or resumes and taking any required tests. If, for example, you are interested in public safety work, make direct contact with police and fire departments at the town, city, or county levels. Many of these local governmental units are very military-friendly (disproportionately staffed with military veterans) and most will have a website with information on their application procedures. Also, consider attending military-friendly job fairs, which often include representatives from police departments that are eager to hire transitioning military personnel.

Websites

Some useful websites include: www.lawenforcementjobs.com, www.policeemployment.com, www.911hotjobs.com, www.officer.com/jobs, and www.theblueline.com.

For a list of Federal employment resource links and a step-by-step Federal Employment Checklist. visit www.CorporateGray.com and click on the Transition Guide tab.

chapter 9

Conduct Research in Key Areas

THE OLD ADAGE THAT "knowledge is power" is especially true when conducting a job search. Your job search is only as good as the knowledge you acquire and use for finding the job you want. Gathering, processing, and using information is the lifeblood of any job search. Research integrates the individual job search activities and provides feedback for adapting strategies to the realities of the job market. Given the numerous individuals and organizations involved in your job search, you must develop an information gathering strategy that will help you gain knowledge about, as well as access to, those individuals and organizations that will play the most important role in your job search.

Research Purposes

Research is the key to gathering, processing, and using information in your job search. It is a skill that will point you in fruitful directions for minimizing job search frustrations and maximizing successes. Be sure to make research one of your top priorities in your job search campaign.

You know from your military experience how important gathering intelligence data is to military operations. Those units that invested the time and energy to properly prepare for an exercise were the most successful. While your job search setting is different, the principle is the same. The more you know about the companies you're interested in, the higher the probability you will succeed in obtaining the job you seek. The knowledge you gain from your in-depth research will give you a competitive advantage over those less well prepared. And that's the force multiplier you want, right?

Most people are reluctant to initiate a research campaign which involves using libraries, computers, and telephoning and meeting new people. Such reluctance is due in part to the lack of knowledge on how to conduct research and where to find resources, and in part to a certain cultural shyness which inhibits individuals from initiating contacts with strangers. However, research is not a difficult process. After all, most people conduct research daily as they read and converse with others about problems. This daily research process needs to be specific and focused on your job search campaign.

Research serves several purposes when adapted to your job search. First, knowing the who, what, when, and where of organizations and individuals is essential for targeting your resume and conducting informational and job interviews. Second, the research component should broaden your perspective on the job market in relationship to your motivated abilities and skills and job objective. Since there are over 13,000 different job titles as well as several million job markets, even a full-time research campaign will uncover only a small segment of the job market relevant to your interests and skills.

A third purpose of research is to better understand how to relate your motivated abilities and skills to specific jobs and work environments. Once you research and understand the critical requirements of a given job in a specific work environment, you can assess the appropriateness of that job for you vis-a-vis your pattern of motivated abilities and skills.

Research brings structure and understanding to the chaotic job market.

Fourth, researching organizations and individuals should result in systematically uncovering a set of contacts for developing your job search network. One of your major research goals should be to compile names, addresses, and telephone numbers of individuals who may become important resources in your new network of job contacts.

A fifth purpose of research is to learn the "languages" of alternative jobs and careers. This is especially important if you are leaving the military after many years of service. You can learn to better converse in these languages by reading trade journals, annual reports, pamphlets, and other organizational literature as well as talking with people in various occupational fields. Knowing these languages—especially asking and answering intelligent questions in the language of the employer—is important for conducting successful referral and job interviews.

Finally, research should result in bringing some degree of structure, coherence, and understanding to the inherently decentralized, fragmented, and chaotic job market. Without research, you place yourself at the mercy of chance and luck; thus, you become a subject of your environment. Research best enables you to take control of your situation. It is power. Your research activities should focus on four major targets: occupational alternatives, organizations, individuals, and communities. If you give equal time to all four, you will be well on your way to getting job interviews and offers.

Use Military Resources

Since this may be the first time you've looked for a civilian job, you need to properly research the job market by acquainting yourself with the right career resources. We recommend starting with the reference library in your local Transition Assistance Program office. There you will find career-related books, magazines, trade publications, and information on employers who have demonstrated interest in hiring former military. They will likely have networked computers that will enable you to "let your fingers do the walking" by accessing employment-related websites, including those that are military-focused. We recommend taking full advantage of these free, yet valuable services. In addition to using the resources available through the TAP offices, we also recommend using your base library. Many base libraries have put together excellent collections of career resources, from key directories to job search books for your use. During the past few years these centers have acquired a wide array of career resources to assist service personnel and their spouses in their transition. Many have key directories, job search books, videos, and computer software for conducting job searches. More importantly, they are staffed with people knowledgeable about the career transition process and willing to assist you in your transition to the civilian work world.

Investigate Alternative Jobs and Careers

Your initial research should help familiarize you with job and career alternatives. For example, the U.S. Department of Labor identifies approximately 13,000 job titles. Most individuals are occupationally illiterate and unaware of the vast array of available jobs and careers. Therefore, it is essential to investigate occupational alternatives in order to broaden your perspective on the job market. As a member of the military, it is especially important for you to discover how your military job skills and titles best correspond to specific civilian job skills and titles. You might start by looking at the VMET form we discussed in Chapter 4. After that, you should start your research by examining several key directories that provide information on alternative jobs and careers:

- *The Occupational Outlook Handbook* (www.bls.gov/oco)
- *The O*NET Dictionary of Occupational Titles* (http://online.onetcenter.org)

You will also find several books that focus on alternative jobs and careers. NTC Publishing and Peterson's, for example, publish more than 200 books on alternative jobs and careers. Several companies also produce computer software programs and CD-ROMs that explore different careers.

Research Electronically

In addition to the traditional resource materials discussed above, we strongly recommend doing research electronically using the Web. By accessing the Web and using popular search engines like Google (www.google.com), Yahoo (www.yahoo.com), and Bing (www.Bing.com) you can quickly gain access to a wealth of information about jobs and careers—either from the privacy of your home or using the computer services available through your local TAP office.

Using a search engine like Google, you can enter the name of a career, industry, company or just about anything else you would like, and bingo—within seconds you have the response to your query. Let's say, for example, that you are interested in Lockheed Martin or any of the employment sponsors listed in the Employment and Services section. Simply type the name of the firm in the text box and press the "OK" or "start" button. The search engine software will quickly find "hits" on the company name you entered. Most likely, one of these sites will contain the address for Lockheed Martin's home page. Given that almost all of America's large companies (and most smaller to mid-size companies) are now on the Web, this is an easy, cost-effective way to find valuable information about companies or industries in which you are interested.

For additional information regarding electronic research, see "Conduct Library and Online Research" in Chapter 6.

Target Organizations

After completing research on occupational alternatives, you should identify specific organizations which you are interested in learning more about. Next compile lists of names, addresses, and telephone numbers of important individuals in each organization. Also, write and telephone the organizations for information, such as an annual report and recruiting literature. The most important information you should be gathering concerns the organizations' goals, structures, functions, problems, and projected future opportunities and development. Since you will be investing part of your life in such organizations, treat them as you would a potential stock market investment. Compare and evaluate different organizations.

Various directories will assist you in researching organizations. Most are found in the reference sections of libraries:

- *America's Corporate Families and International Affiliates*
- *Consultants and Consulting Organizations Directory*
- *Corporate Technology Directory*
- *Directory of American Firms Operating in Foreign Countries*
- *The Directory of Corporate Affiliations: Who Owns Whom*
- *Dun & Bradstreet's Billion Dollar Directory*
- *Dun & Bradstreet's Middle Market Directory*
- *Dun & Bradstreet's Million Dollar Directory*
- *Dun's Career Guide*
- *Encyclopedia of Business Information Sources*
- *Encyclopedia of Information Services and Agencies*
- *Fitch's Corporation Reports*
- *MacRae's Blue Book*
- *Moody's Manuals*
- *The Multinational Marketing and Employment Directory*
- *O'Dwyer's Directory of Corporate Communications*
- *Standard & Poor's Industrial Index*
- *Standard Rate and Data Business Publications Directory*
- *Thomas' Register of American Manufacturers*
- *Ward's Business Directory of U.S. Private & Public Companies*
- *World Business Directory*

If you are interested in jobs with a particular organization, you should visit their websites to learn about the types of jobs being offered. You may be able to examine vacancy announcements which describe the duties and responsibilities of specific jobs. If you are interested in working for federal, state, or local governments, each agency's personnel office can supply you with a list of vacancies.

Many directories and information services can now be accessed electronically. Again, we recommend starting with the Web (see Chapter 6 for specific sites). As discussed above, you can quickly gain a wealth of information from this ever growing knowledge base.

Contact Individuals

While examining directories, reading books, and surfing the Web on alternative jobs and careers will provide you with useful job search information, much of this material may be too general for specifying the right job for you. In the end, the best information will come directly from people in specific jobs in specific organizations. To get this information you must communicate with knowledgeable people. You especially want to learn more about the people who make the hiring decisions.

You might begin your investigations by contacting various professional and trade associations for detailed information on jobs and careers relevant to their members. And if you wish to contact some of your former military friends who may now be hiring managers or just good networking contacts in the civilian work world, try:

- GI Search (www.gisearch.com)
- Veteran Career Network (http://benefits.military.com/vcn/search.do)
- Vet Friends (www.vetfriends.com)
- Military USA (www.militaryusa.com)
- LinkedIn (www.LinkedIn.com)
- Facebook (www.facebook.com)

Ask the Right Questions

The quality of your research will only be as good as the questions you ask. Therefore, you should focus on a few key questions that will yield useful information for guiding your job search. Answers to these questions will help make important job search decisions relevant to informational and job interviews.

"Who Has the Power to Hire?"

Finding out who has the power to hire may take some research effort on your part. Keep in mind that Human Resources offices normally do not have the power to hire. They handle much of the paperwork involved in announcing vacancies, taking applications, testing candidates, screening credentials, and placing new employees on the payroll. In other words, Human Resources offices tend to perform auxiliary support functions for those who do the actual hiring—usually individuals in the operating business units.

If you want to learn who really has the power to hire, you need to conduct research on the particular operating unit that interests you. You should ask specific questions concerning who normally is responsible for various parts of the hiring process:

- Who describes the positions?
- Who announces vacancies?
- Who receives applications?
- Who administers tests?
- Who selects eligible candidates?
- Who interviews the candidates?
- Who makes the hiring decision?

If you ask these questions about a specific position you will quickly identify who has what powers to hire. Chances are the power to hire is shared between the Human Resources office and the operating unit. You should not neglect the Human Resources office, and in some cases it will play a powerful role in all aspects of the hiring. Your research will reveal to what degree the hiring function has been centralized, decentralized, or fragmented in the organization.

"How Does Organization X Operate?"

It's best to know something about the internal operation of an organization before joining it. But the type of knowledge we recommend you seek goes far beyond the structure of the company or knowledge about its products and services. Yes, these are important and we encourage you to know them. However, the more challenging aspect of your research is to learn about the organization's corporate culture. An organization's corporate culture refers to the overall environment or climate that exists within an organization. Some organizations are high-pressure, where there is an ever present demand to increase the pace of business and profitability, regardless of the human toll. Other organizations might be more laid-back, where the emphasis is on refining the quality of a product or service rather than the amount of business each person is generating. A company's corporate culture permeates the organization. It reflects the values and morals of the organization's senior leaders. If they make it clear that unacceptable behavior will not be tolerated and they "walk the talk," chances are the rank-and-file will get the message and behave accordingly. In many ways, you are already familiar with a corporate culture—your service's. Your research into prospective companies should help you determine whether you'll fit in to their corporate culture. When possible, we suggest trying to solicit this information in your informational interviews. It often takes several months before you fully appreciate the corporate culture and by that time, it might be too late.

There are many other, more pragmatic reasons for conducting a thorough research of prospective companies. Your research may uncover information that would convince you that a particular organization is not one in which you wish to invest your time and effort. You may learn, for example, that Company X has a history of terminating employees before they become vested in the company retirement system. Or Company X may be experiencing serious financial problems.

You can get financial information about most companies by examining their annual reports as well as by talking to individuals who know the organization well. To obtain a copy of a publicly owned company's annual report, simply call and ask. Most will give you a free copy. If, on the other hand, the company is privately owned, they will probably decline your request. With regard to information on internal operations, especially company politics and power, you must glean this information from individuals who work within the organization. Ask them: "Is this a good organization to work for?" and let them expand on specific areas you wish to probe—advancement opportunities, working conditions, relationships among co-workers and supervisors, growth patterns, internal politics, management styles, work values, opportunities for taking initiative.

"What Do I Need to Do to Get a Job With Organization X?"

The best way to find how to get a job in a particular organization is to follow the advice in the next chapter on prospecting, networking, and informational interviewing. This question can only be answered by talking to people who know formal and informal hiring practices.

You can get information on the formal hiring system by contacting the Human Resources office. A telephone call should be sufficient to get this information.

But you must go beyond the formal system and Human Resources office in order to learn how best to conduct your job search. This means contacting people who know how one really gets hired in the organization. The best sources of information will be individuals who play a major role in the hiring process.

Locate Job Vacancies

While most people tend to look to the classified section of the newspaper for job listings, be sure to investigate other sources for vacancy announcements.

One of the best sources of information for current job vacancies is the Internet. In Chapter 8, we listed some of the largest employment websites. In addition, many companies now have their own database of job openings. In fact, many of these companies enable you to submit your resume online.

To locate federal job vacancies, visit: OPM (www.usajobs.opm.gov), Federal Research Service (www.fedjobs.com), and Federal Jobs Digest (www.jobsfed.com). You should also access Career OneStop (www.CareerOneStop.org/MilitaryTransition). Many of the Federal job openings will give veterans' preference. And don't overlook trade and professional associations. For excellent online directories of professional associations, visit these two sites: http://www.ipl.org/div/aon/ and www.asaenet.org.

Identify the Right Community

Your final research target is central to all other research targets and it may occur at any stage in your research. As you separate or retire from the service, identifying the geographical area where you would like to work will be one of your most important career decisions. Once you make this decision, other job search decisions and activities become easier. For example, if you separate in a small town, you may need to move to a larger community which offers more opportunities for career changers. If you are a member of a two-career family, opportunities for both you and your spouse will be greater in a growing metropolitan area. If you plan to relocate to another community, you will need to develop a long-distance job search campaign which has different characteristics than a local campaign. It will probably involve much correspondence, time perusing various employment sites on the Internet, long-distance phone calls, and possibly even visits to those communities in which you have the most interest. If you want to explore various communities, you should examine several of these gateway community sites:

- Boulevards www.boulevards.com
- City-Data www.city-data.com
- City Travel Guide www.citytravelguide.com
- Cities.com www.cities.com
- Tourism Offices Worldwide Directory www.towd.com
- USA City Link www.usacitylink.com
- Yahoo http://realestate.yahoo.com/neighborhoods

Arranged alphabetically, each listing includes company name, address, phone number; SIC code; number of employees; annual revenues; the name of the key personnel executive; and names of other human resources staff. Your most productive research activity will be communicating with people by phone, fax, or e-mail, and in face-to-face meetings. Informal, word-of-mouth communication is still the most effective channel of job search information. In contrast to reading books, people have more current, detailed, and accurate information. Ask them about:

- Occupational fields
- Job requirements and training
- Interpersonal environments
- Performance expectations
- Their problems
- Salaries
- Advancement opportunities
- Future growth potential of the organization
- Best way to acquire more information and contacts

You may be surprised how willingly friends, acquaintances, and strangers will give you useful information. But before you talk to people, do your library research so that you are better able to ask thoughtful questions and appear well informed.

Forfurther assistance in conducting company research and for a checklist of links to online resources, visit www.CorporateGray.com and click on the Transition Guide tab.

chapter 10

Network Your Way to Career Success

NOW THAT YOU HAVE IDENTIFIED your skills, specified your objective, written your resume, and conducted research, what should you do next? At this point let's examine where you are going so you don't get preoccupied with the trees and thus lose sight of the larger forest. Let's identify the most effective methods for linking your previous job search activities to job interviews and offers. In so doing, you'll be well prepared to land a job.

Focus on Getting Interviews

Everything you have done to this point in your job search should be aimed at getting a job interview. The skills you identified, the goals you set, the resume you wrote, and the information you gathered are carefully related to one another so you will have maximum impact communicating your qualifications to employers, who, in turn, will decide to invite you to a job interview.

But there are secrets to getting a job interview you should know before continuing further with your job search. The most important secret is the informational interview—a type of interview which yields useful job search information and may lead to job interviews and offers. Based on prospecting and networking techniques, these interviews minimize rejections and competition as well as quickly open the doors to organizations and employers. If you want a job interview, you first need to understand the informational interview and how to initiate and use it effectively.

Prospecting and Networking

What do you do after you complete your resume? Most people send cover letters and resumes in response to job listings; they then wait to be called for a job interview. Viewing the job search as basically a direct-mail operation, many are disappointed in discovering the realities of direct-mail—a 5-percent response rate is considered outstanding! Successful job seekers break out of this relatively passive job search role by orienting themselves toward face-to-face action. Being proactive, they develop interpersonal strategies in which the resume plays a supportive rather than a central role in the job search. They first present themselves to employers; the resume appears only at the end of a face-to-face meeting.

Throughout the job search you will acquire useful names and addresses as well as meet people who will assist you in contacting potential employers. Such information and contacts become key building blocks for generating job interviews and offers.

Since the best and most numerous jobs are found in the hidden job market, you must use methods appropriate for this job market. Indeed, research and experience clearly show the most effective means of communication are face-to-face and word-of-mouth. The informal, interpersonal system of communication is the central nervous system of the hidden job market. Your goal should be to penetrate this job market with proven methods for success. Appropriate methods for making important job contacts are **prospecting** and **networking**. Appropriate methods for getting these contacts to provide you with useful job information are **informational** and **referral interviews**.

Communicate Your Qualifications

Taken together, these interpersonal methods help you **communicate your qualifications** to employers. Although many job seekers may be reluctant to use this informal communication system, they greatly limit their potential for success if they do not.

Put yourself in the position of the employer for a moment. You have a job vacancy to fill. If you advertise the position, you may be bombarded with hundreds of resumes, applications, phone calls, faxes, and walk-ins. While you do want to hire the best qualified individual for the job, you simply don't have time or patience to review scores of applications. Even if you use a P.O. Box number, the paperwork may quickly overwhelm you. Furthermore, with limited information from application forms, cover letters, and resumes, you find it hard to identify the best qualified individuals to invite for an interview; many look the same on paper.

So, as an employer what do you do? You might use a military search firm to take on all of this additional work. On the other hand, you may want to better control the hiring process, especially since it appears to be filled with uncertainty and headaches. You want to minimize your risks and time so you can get back to what you do best—accomplishing the external goals of the organization. Like many other employers, you begin by calling your friends, acquaintances, and other business associates and ask if they or someone else might know of any good candidates for the position. If they can't help, you ask them to give you a call should they learn of anyone qualified for your vacancy. You, in effect, create your own hidden job market—an informal information network for locating desirable candidates. Your trusted contacts initially screen the candidates in the process of referring them to you. This both saves you time and minimizes your risks in hiring a stranger.

Based on this understanding of the employer's perspective, what should you do to best improve your chances of getting an interview and job offer? Networking for information, advice, and referrals should play a central role in your overall job search. Remember, employers need to solve personnel problems. By conducting informational interviews and networking, you help employers identify their needs, limit their alternatives, and thus make decisions and save money. Most important, such networking activities help relieve their anxiety of hiring a career changer. At the same time, you gain several advantages by conducting these interviews:

1. You are less likely to encounter rejections since you are not asking for a job—only information, advice, and referrals.
2. You go after unadvertised positions.
3. You encounter little competition.
4. You go directly to the people who have the power to hire.
5. You are likely to be invited to interviews based upon the referrals you receive.

Most employers want more information on candidates to supplement the "paper qualifications" represented in application forms, resumes, and letters. Studies show that employers in general seek candidates who have these skills: communication, problem solving, analytical, assessment, and planning. Surprising to many job seekers, technical expertise ranks third or fourth on employers' lists of most desired skills. These findings support a frequent observation made by employers: the major problems with employees relate to communication, problem solving, and analysis; individuals get fired because of political and interpersonal conflicts rather than technical incompetence.

Employers seek individuals they like both personally and professionally. Therefore, communicating your qualifications to employers entails more than just informing them of your technical competence. You must communicate that you have the requisite personal and professional skills for performing the job. Informal prospecting, networking, and informational interviewing activities are the best methods for communicating your "qualifications" to employers.

Develop Networks

Networking is the process of purposefully developing relations with others. Networking in the job search involves connecting and interacting with other individuals who can be helpful to you. Your network consists of everyone with whom you interact. The more you develop, maintain, and expand your networks, the more successful your job search should be.

Your network is your interpersonal environment. While you know and interact with hundreds of people, on a day-to-day basis you may encounter no more than 20 people. You frequently contact these people in face-to-face situations. Some people are more important to you than others. You like some more than others. And some will be more helpful to you in your job search than others.

As a member of the military, you already have an extensive network in place. Based on your many moves and the scores of people you have come in contact with through your military service, you should be well positioned to take advantage of this important employment avenue. It's now time to begin networking your way to career transition success.

Your most important network may be your military contacts—both those still in the military and those who have separated or retired. This is not the time to be bashful. You need to let your military colleagues know that you are actively searching for a job. You will be pleasantly surprised by the positive response you will receive. Indeed, the military tends to be a close knit family that looks out for each other. Military friends and associates who have already transitioned to the private sector can be especially helpful, for they know first-hand where the hidden jobs are within their organizations. You might want to begin by referring to your holiday card list or by using the worldwide locator service of your military service to identify where all of your old friends and colleagues are now located. You also should join various military associations (see Chapter 3) where you can make important professional contacts. And don't forget to use social media tools like LinkedIn and Twitter (see page 107) where where you can network virtually!

Your basic network will encompass the following individuals and groups: friends, acquaintances, immediate family, distant relatives, professional colleagues, spouse, supervisor, fellow workers, close friends and colleagues, and local businessmen and professionals, such as your banker, lawyer, doctor, minister, and insurance agent. You should contact many of these individuals for advice relating to your job search.

You need to identify everyone in your network who might help you with your job search. You first need to expand your basic network to include individuals you know and have interacted with over the past 10 or more years. Make a list of at least 200 people you know. Include friends and relatives, past and present neighbors, former classmates, politicians, business persons, previous employers, professional associates, ministers, insurance agents, lawyers, bankers, doctors, dentists, accountants, and social acquaintances.

After identifying your extended network, you should try to link your network to others' networks. The figure below illustrates this linkage principle. Individuals in these other networks also have job information and contacts. Ask people in your basic network for referrals. This approach should greatly enlarge your basic job search network.

Linking Your Networks to Others

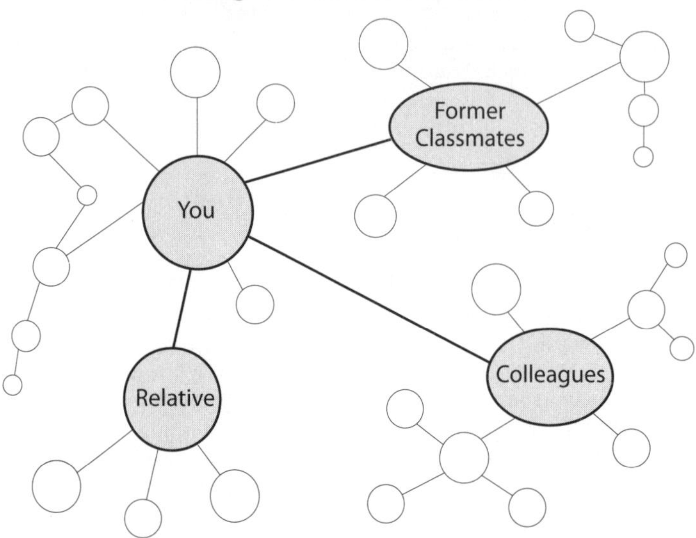

What do you do if individuals in your immediate and extended network cannot provide you with certain job information and contacts? While it is much easier and more effective to meet new people through personal contacts, on occasion you may need to approach strangers without prior contacts. In this situation, try the "cold turkey" approach. Write a letter to someone you feel may be useful to your job search. Research this individual so you are acquainted with their background and accomplishments. In the letter, refer to their accomplishments, mention your need for job information, and specify a date and time you will call to schedule a meeting. Another approach is to introduce yourself to someone by telephone and request a meeting and/or job information. While you may experience rejections in using these approaches, you also will experience successes. And those successes should lead to further expansion of your job search network.

Online Networking

Online networking is increasingly becoming an important communications medium in today's high-tech environment. Job seekers have worldwide access to others through online services, such as Yahoo, as well as via the Internet. All of these online services have newsgroups, or electronic "town halls," where you can "chat" on topics of mutual interest. These newsgroups are normally organized around a central theme or topic. At the same time, you may want to contact your former military buddies through these websites:

- www.GISearch.com
- /www.military.com/buddy-finder/
- www.vetfriends.com
- www.militaryusa.com

Social Networking Media

The use of social media has exploded in recent years and can be used in your job search. By leveraging the power of the Internet, you can extend your networking activities through tools such as LinkedIn.com, Twitter, Facebook, and MySpace. By mastering the use of these electronic tools, you will maximize the chances of your friends—and people you may not yet know but share a common interest—helping you identify job leads.

LinkedIn is a professional networking tool that helps you stay in contact with past and present colleagues, find job opportunities, identify key individuals within companies of interest, and then use your connections to be introduced and, hopefully, get the job. If you have not yet created a LinkedIn account, we encourage you to do so. Make sure to fully complete your profile and give special attention to the Headline. By making it enticing, you make it more likely that will someone—like a recruiter— will want to contact you. LinkedIn also has Status Updates, and we suggest you update your status from time-to-time so that your connections stay apprised of your job search progress. Most importantly, LinkedIn supports Groups. We suggest joining and participating in military-affiliated Groups, especially those concerning military-to-civilian career transition.

In addition to identifying jobs and networking with key individuals within various companies, LinkedIn also gives you the ability to link your blog post or Twitter page to your profile. Why is that important? Because every time you enter a new blog post or tweet someone, that information will be sent to your LinkedIn connections, which will keep your job search fresh in their mind!

Twitter allows you to network with people you may not know but share a common interest. When you send someone a message using Twitter, it's called a tweet. Tweets are quick, bite-sized (no more than 140 characters) comments. By tweeting people in your shared neighborhood of common interests, you will likely soon learn about job openings at companies of mutual interest and, through tweets with your new friends, gain insight into those jobs. Be proactive, connect with as many people as appropriate.

Facebook is a tool for primarily connecting with friends and reconnecting with people from your past. It, too, can be an effective networking tool. For example, you might post a "note" on Facebook letting people know that you are leaving the military and seeking civilian employment. In addition to notes, Facebook also lets you give a Status Update. By frequently updating your status, you are enabling those who visit your Facebook page to stay current with what's happening in your life. And, of course, you will want to include the status of your job search so that they have the latest information. If you write a blog post, create a note for it. And if your blog post references a friend on Facebook, tag them so that your friends will be alerted to your post, and your message will spread more quickly.

You also may want to take advantage of formal online networking groups such as:

- ExecuNet www.execunet.com
- Company of friends http://fastcompany.com/cof
- Friendster www.friendster.com

Given the wide expanse of these online networks, you now have access to a global network of potential contacts—at a minimal cost. Online networking is especially useful for those stationed overseas, who are at a disadvantage with regard to face-to-face networking.

For information on the latest strategies for using social media in your job search, check out these three books, which are available through www.impactpublications.com: *Find a Job Through Social Networking*; *How to Find a Job on LinkedIn, Facebook, Twitter, MySpace, and Other Social Networks*; and *Twitter Job Search Guide*.

Prospect For Leads

The key to successful networking is an active and routine prospecting campaign. Salespersons in insurance, real estate, and other direct-sales businesses understand the importance and principles of prospecting. Indeed, many have turned the art of prospecting into a science! The basic operating principle is probability: the number of sales you make is a direct function of the amount of effort you put into developing new contacts and following through. Expect no more than a 10-percent acceptance rate: for every 10 people you meet, nine will reject you and one will accept you. Therefore, the more people you contact, the more acceptances you will receive. If you want to be successful, you must collect many more "no's" than "yeses." In a 10-percent probability situation, you need to contact 100 people for 10 successes.

These prospecting principles are extremely useful for making a career change. Like sales situations, the job search is a highly ego-involved activity often characterized by numerous rejections accompanied by a few acceptances. While no one wants to be rejected, few people are willing or able to handle more than a few rejections. They take a "no" as a sign of personal failure—and quit prematurely. If they persisted longer, they would achieve success after a few more "no's." Furthermore, if their prospecting activities were focused on gathering information rather than making sales, they would considerably minimize the number of rejections. Therefore, you should do the following:

- Prospect for job leads.
- Accept rejections as part of the game.
- Link prospecting to informational interviewing.
- Keep prospecting for more information and "yeses" which will eventually translate into job interviews and offers.

A good prospecting pace as you start your search is to make two new contacts each day. Start by contacting people in your immediate network. Let them know you are conducting a job search, but emphasize that you are only doing research. Ask for a few moments of their time to discuss your information needs. You are only seeking information and advice at this time—not a job.

It should take you about 20 minutes to make a contact by letter or telephone. If you make two contacts each day, by the end of the first week you will have 10 new contacts for a total investment of less than seven hours. By the second week you may want to increase your prospecting pace to four new contacts each day or 20 each week. The more contacts you make, the more useful information, advice, and job leads you will receive. If your job search bogs down, you probably need to increase your prospecting activities. Expect each contact to refer you to two or three others who will also refer you to others.

Handle and Minimize Rejections

These prospecting and networking methods are effective. While they are responsible for building, maintaining, and expanding multimillion-dollar businesses, they work extremely well for job hunters. But they only work if you are patient and persist. The key to networking success is to focus on gathering information while also learning to handle rejections. Learn from rejections, forget them, and go on to more productive networking activities.

The major reason direct-sales people fail is because they don't persist. The reason they don't persist is because they either can't take, or get tired of taking, rejections.

Rejections are no fun, especially in such an ego-involved activity as a job search. But you will likely encounter rejections as you travel on the road toward job search success. This road is strewn with individuals who quit prematurely because they were rejected four or five times. Don't be one of them!

Our prospecting and networking techniques differ from sales approaches in one major respect: we have special techniques for minimizing the number of rejections. If handled properly, at least 50 percent—maybe as many as 90 percent—of your prospects will turn into "yeses" rather than "no's." The reason for this unusually high acceptance rate is how you introduce and handle yourself before your prospects. Many sales agents and direct distributors expect a 90-percent rejection rate, because they are trying to sell specific products potential clients may or may not need. Most people don't like to be put on the spot—especially when it's in their home or office—to make a decision to buy a product.

Be Honest and Sincere

The principles of selling yourself in the job market are similar. People don't want to be put on the spot. They feel uncomfortable if they think you expect them to give you a job. Thus, you should never introduce yourself to a prospect by asking them for a job or a job lead. You should do just the opposite: relieve their anxiety by mentioning that you are not looking for a job from them—only job information and advice. You must be honest and sincere in communicating these intentions to your contact. The biggest turnoff for individuals targeted for informational interviews is insincere job seekers who try to use this as a mechanism to get a job.

Your approach to prospects must be sincere, honest, and professional. You are seeking information, advice, and referrals relating to several subjects: job opportunities, your job search approach, your resume, and contacts who may have similar information, advice, and referrals. Most people gladly volunteer such information. They generally like to talk about themselves, their careers, and others. They like to give advice. This approach flatters individuals by placing them in the role of the expert advisor. Who doesn't want to be recognized as an expert advisor, especially on such a critical topic as one's employment?

This approach should yield a great deal of information, advice, and referrals from your prospects. One other important outcome should result from using this approach: people will remember you as the person who made them feel at ease and who received their valuable advice. If they hear of job opportunities for someone with your qualifications, chances are they will pass the information on to you. After contacting 100 prospects, you will have created 100 sets of eyes and ears to help you in your job search!

Practice the 5 Rs of Informational Interviewing

The guiding principle behind prospecting, networking, and informational interviews is this: **the best way to get a job is to ask for job information, advice, and referrals; never ask for a job.** Remember, you want your prospects to engage in the 5 Rs of informational interviewing:

- **Reveal** useful information and advice.
- **Refer** you to others.
- **Read** your resume.
- **Revise** your resume.
- **Remember** you for future reference.

If you follow this principle, you should join the ranks of many successful job seekers.

Approach Key People

Whom should you contact within an organization for an informational interview? Contact people who are busy, who have the power to hire, and who are knowledgeable about the organization. The least likely candidate will be someone in the personnel department. Most often the heads of operating units are the most busy, powerful, and knowledgeable individuals in the organization. However, getting access to such individuals may be difficult. Some people at the top may appear to be informed and powerful, but they may lack information on the day-to-day personnel changes, or their knowledge is limited in the hiring process. It is difficult to give one best answer to this question.

Therefore, we recommend contacting several types of people. Aim for the busy, powerful, and informed, but be prepared to settle for less. Secretaries, receptionists, and the person you want to meet may refer you to others. From a practical standpoint, you may have to take whomever you can schedule an appointment with. Sometimes people who are less powerful can be helpful. Talk to a secretary or receptionist sometime about their boss or working in the organization. You may be surprised at what you learn!

Nonetheless, you will conduct informational interviews with different types of people. Some will be friends, relatives, or acquaintances. Others will be referrals or new contacts. You will gain the easiest access to people you already know. This can usually be done informally by telephone. You might meet at their home or office or at a restaurant.

You should use a more formal approach to gain access to referrals and new contacts. The best way to initiate a contact with a prospective employer is to send an approach letter and follow it up with a phone call. Examples of approach letters are found at the end of Chapter 7. This letter should include the following elements:

1. **OPENING:** If you have a referral, tell the individual you are considering a career in ________. His or her name was given to you by ________ who suggested he or she might be a good person to give you useful information about careers in ________. Should you lack a referral to the individual and thus must use a "cold turkey" approach to making this contact, you might begin your letter by stating that you are aware he or she has been at the forefront of ________ business—or whatever is both truthful and appropriate for the situation. A subtle form of flattery will be helpful at this stage.

2. **REQUEST:** Demonstrate your thoughtfulness and courtesy rather than aggressiveness by mentioning that you know he or she is busy. You hope to schedule a mutually convenient time for a brief meeting to discuss your questions and career plans. Most people will be flattered by such a request and happy to talk with you about their work—if they have time and are interested.

3. **CLOSING:** In closing the letter, mention that you will call the person to see if an appointment can be arranged. Be specific by stating the time and day you will call—for example, Thursday at 2pm. You must take initiative to follow up the letter with a definite contact time. If you don't, you cannot expect to hear from the person. It is your responsibility to make the telephone call to schedule a meeting.

4. **ENCLOSURE:** Do NOT enclose your resume with this approach letter. You should take your resume to the interview and present it as a topic of discussion near the end of your meeting. If you send it with the approach letter, you communicate a mixed and contradictory message. Remember your purpose for this interview: to gather information and advice. You are NOT—and never should be—asking for a job. A resume accompanying a letter appears to be an application or a job request.

Many people will meet with you, assuming you are sincere in your approach. On the other hand, many people also are very busy and simply don't have the time to meet with you. If the person puts you off when you telephone for an appointment, clearly state your purpose and emphasize that you are not looking for a job with this person—only information and advice. If the person persists in putting you off, make the best of the situation: try to conduct the informational interview over the telephone. Alternatively, write a nice thank-you letter in which you again state your intended purpose, mention your disappointment in not being able to learn from the person's experience, and ask to be remembered for future reference. Enclose your resume with this letter.

While you are ostensibly seeking information and advice, treat this meeting as an important preliminary interview. You need to communicate your qualifications—that you are competent, intelligent, honest, and likable. These are the same qualities you should communicate in a formal job interview. Hence, follow the same advice given for conducting a formal interview and dressing appropriately for a face-to-face meeting.

Conduct the Interview Well

An informational interview will be relatively unstructured compared to a formal job interview. Since you want the interviewer to advise you, you reverse roles by asking questions which should give you useful information. You, in effect, become the interviewer. You should structure this interview with a particular sequence of questions. Most questions should be open-ended, requiring the individual to give specific answers based upon his or her experiences.

The structure and dialogue for the informational interview might go something like this. You plan to take no more than 45 minutes for this interview. The first three to five minutes will be devoted to small talk—the weather, traffic, the office, mutual acquaintances, or an interesting or humorous observation. Since these are the most critical moments in the interview, be especially careful how you communicate nonverbally. Begin your interview by stating your appreciation for the individual's time:

> *"I want to thank you again for scheduling this meeting with me. I know you're busy. I appreciate the special arrangements you made to see me on a subject which is very important to my future."*

Next, you should reiterate your purpose as stated in your letter:

> *"As you know, I am exploring job and career alternatives. I know what I do well and what I want to do. But before I commit myself to a new job, I need to know more about various career options. I thought you would be able to provide me with some insights into career opportunities, job requirements, and possible problems or promising directions in the field of ____________."*

This statement normally will get a positive reaction from the individual who may want to know more about what it is you want to do. Be sure to clearly communicate your job objective. If you can't, you may communicate that you are lost, indecisive, or uncertain about yourself. The person may feel you are wasting his or her time.

Your next line of questioning should focus on "how" and "what" questions centering on (1) specific jobs and (2) the job search process. Begin by asking about various aspects of specific jobs:

- Duties and responsibilities
- Knowledge, skills, and abilities required
- Work environment relating to fellow employees, work flows, deadlines, stress, initiative
- Advantages and disadvantages
- Advancement opportunities and outlook
- Salary ranges

Your informer will probably take a great deal of time talking about his or her experience in each area. Be a good listener, but make sure you move along with the questions.

Your next line of questioning should focus on your job search activities. You need as much information as possible on how to:

- Acquire the necessary skills
- Best find a job in this field
- Overcome any objections employers may have to you
- Uncover job vacancies which may not be advertised
- Develop job leads
- Approach prospective employers

Your final line of questioning should focus on your resume. Do not show your resume until you address this last set of questions. The purpose of these questions is to: (1) get the individual to read your resume in depth, (2) acquire useful advice on how to strengthen it, (3) get a referral to prospective employers, and (4) be remembered. With the resume in front of you and your interviewee, ask the following questions:

- Is this an appropriate type of resume for the jobs I have outlined?
- If an employer received this resume in the mail, how do you think he or she would react to it?
- What do you see as possible weaknesses or areas that need to be improved?
- What should I do with this resume? Shotgun it to hundreds of employers with a cover letter? Use resume letters instead?
- What about the length, paper quality and color, layout, and typing? Are they appropriate?
- How might I improve the form and content of the resume?

You should receive useful advice on how to strengthen both the content and use of your resume. Most important, these questions force the individual to read your resume which, in turn, may be remembered for future reference.

Your last question is especially important in this interview. You want to be both remembered and referred. Some variation of the following question should help:

> *"I really appreciate all this advice. It is very helpful and it should improve my job search considerably. Could I ask you one more favor? Do you know two or three other people who could help me with my job search? I want to conduct as much research as possible, and their advice might be helpful also."*

Before you leave, mention one more important item:

> *"During the next few months, should you hear of any job opportunities for someone with my interests and qualifications, I would appreciate being kept in mind. And please feel free to pass my name on to others."*

Send a nice thank-you letter within 48 hours of completing this informational interview. Express your genuine gratitude for the individual's time and advice. Reiterate your interests, and ask to be remembered and referred to others.

Follow up on any useful advice you receive, particularly referrals. Approach referrals in the same manner you approached the person who gave you the referral. Write a letter requesting a meeting. Begin the letter by mentioning:

> *"Mr./Ms. __________ suggested that I contact you concerning my research on careers in __________."*

If you continue prospecting, networking, and conducting informational interviews, soon you will be busy conducting interviews and receiving job offers. While 100 informational interviews over a two-month period should lead to several formal job interviews and offers, the pay-offs are uncertain because job vacancies are unpredictable. We know cases where the first referral turned into a formal interview and job offer. More typical cases require constant prospecting, networking, and informational interviewing activities. The telephone call or letter inviting you to a job interview can come at any time. While the timing may be unpredictable, your persistent job search activities will be largely responsible for the final outcome.

For more assistance in buildimg your job search network as well as networking etiquette and tips, visit www.CorporateGray.com and click on the Transition Guide tab.

chapter 11

Interview for the Right Job

MAKE NO MISTAKE—the job interview is the most important step in the job search process. All previous job search activities lead to this one. Put simply, no interview, no job offer; no job offer, no negotiations, no salary, and no job.

It's also important that you interview for the right job. By this we mean one that is compatible with your knowledge, skills, interests, and problem solving ability. Only you can judge what constitutes the right job. Just remember—you are starting a new track record. You want to find a job that you will enjoy and do well. Your previous job search activities—informational interviews, research, telephone screening interviews should provide you with a strong indication as to whether a given job is right for you. Let's assume you've done your homework and that you have found an employment opportunity that appears right for you. Now it's time to prepare for the job interview. As we've stressed in previous chapters, proper preparation is key. How you approach the interview will make a difference in the outcome of the interview. Therefore, you need to know what best to do and not to do in order to make an excellent impression on employers.

Interviewing For the Job

Nearly 95 percent of all organizations require job interviews prior to hiring employees. In fact, employers consider an effective interview to be the most important hiring criteria—outranking grade point average, related work experience, and recommendations.

While the job interview is the most important job search activity, it also is the most stressful job search experience. Your application, resume, and letters may get you to the interview, but you must perform well in person in order to get a job offer. Knowing the stakes are high, most people face interviews with dry throats and sweaty palms; it is a time of great stress. You will be on stage, and you are expected to put on a good performance.

How do you prepare for the interview? First, you need to understand the nature and purpose of the interview. Second, you must prepare to respond to the interview situation and the interviewer. Make sure whomever assists you in preparing for the interview evaluates your performance. Practice the whole interviewing scenario, from the time you enter the door until you leave. You should sharpen your nonverbal communication skills and be prepared to give positive answers to questions as well as ask intelligent questions. The more you practice, the better prepared you will be for the real job interview.

Communication

An interview is a two-way communication exchange between an interviewer and interviewee. It involves both verbal and nonverbal communication. While we tend to concentrate on the content of what we say, research shows that approximately 65 percent of all communication is nonverbal. Furthermore, we tend to give more credibility to nonverbal than to verbal messages. Regardless of what you say, how you dress, sit, stand, use your hands, move your head and eyes, and listen communicate both positive and negative messages.

Job interviews can occur in many different settings and under various circumstances. You will write job interview letters, schedule interviews by telephone, be interviewed over the phone, and encounter one-on-one as well as panel, group, and series interviews. Each situation requires a different set of communication behaviors. For example, while telephone communication is efficient, it may be ineffective for interview purposes. Only certain types of information can be effectively communicated over the telephone because this medium limits nonverbal behavior. Honesty, intelligence, and likability—three of the most important values to communicate to employers—are primarily communicated nonverbally. Therefore, you should be very careful of telephone interviews—whether initiating or receiving them.

Job interviews have different purposes and can be negative in many ways. From your perspective, the purpose of an initial job interview is to get a second interview, and the purpose of the second interview is to get a job offer. However, for many employers, the purpose of the interview is to eliminate you from a second interview or job offer. The interviewer wants to know why he or she should not hire you. The interviewer tries to do this by identifying your weaknesses. These differing purposes can create an adversarial relationship and contribute to the overall interviewing stress experienced by both the applicant and the interviewer.

Since the interviewer wants to identify your weaknesses, you must counter by communicating your strengths to lessen the interviewer's fears of hiring you. Recognizing that you are an unknown quantity to the employer, you must raise the interviewer's expectations of you.

Answering Questions

Hopefully your prospecting, networking, informational interviewing, and resume and letter writing activities result in several job interviews appropriate to your objective and background. Once you receive an invitation to interview, you should do a great deal of work in preparation for your meeting. You should prepare for the interview as if it were a $1,000,000 prize. After all, that may be what you earn during your employment.

In today's competitive job market, hiring managers often receive scores of resumes. Consequently, the initial interview will most likely be done over the phone. To make best use of their time, many hiring managers will filter through the stack of resumes and select the five to ten most promising for a phone screen. This telephone interview is an important early discriminator of potential employees, so you must be prepared for it at any time. Knowing that phone screens are important, you can gain a competitive advantage over less motivated job seekers through careful preparation. We recommend you start by developing a telephone script. A script is a series of questions you expect to be asked along with notes on your prepared responses. Examples of the types of questions you might encounter follow:

- What type of work are you looking for?
- What do you consider your strongest skills? Weakest skills?
- How did you hear about this job opportunity?
- What do you know about our company?
- Why are you interested in working for us?
- Do you have a college degree? If so, in what? From where?
- What are your salary expectations?
- What are you doing now?
- Are you willing to relocate?
- Are you willing to travel? How much (what percentage)?
- When would you be available to start work?
- When could you meet with us?

In response to each question, you should develop a clear, concise, well thought out answer. Using a word processor to develop this script will enable you to refine and improve your answers. Then you should practice delivering your response so that you'll be ready to give polished answers in a clear, confident tone. Do not try to memorize answers since they are likely to sound like canned responses. Use this script to trigger appropriate responses that sound both spontaneous and energetic. When you're done with your preparations, we strongly recommend leaving a copy of the script and your resume next to each phone in the house so that regardless of when the hiring manager calls, you'll be ready. Remember, the phone screen is often when the prospective employer will get his first impression of you. Your job is to make it as positive as possible.

Successful telephone interviews often result in a face-to-face interview at the employer's office. Once you confirm an interview time and place, you should do as much research on the organization and employer as possible. Learn to lessen your anxiety and stress levels by practicing the interview situation. Preparation and practice are the keys to doing your best.

During the interview, you want to impress the interviewer by providing brief, to-the-point answers that relate your skills and experience to their needs. Where possible, your answers should blend your knowledge of the firm based on your research and networking activities (Chapters 9 and 10). This is also the time to impress the interviewer with your knowledge of the organization by asking insightful questions. In so doing, you will help the interviewer see you as the right person for the job. Your goal at this stage in the process is to motivate the interviewer to ask you back for a second interview.

You should practice for the interview by mentally addressing several questions most interviewers ask. Most of these questions will relate to your educational background, work experiences, career goals, personality, and related concerns. Some of the most frequently asked questions include:

Education

- Describe your educational background.
- How have you improved your education while in the military?
- Have you started work on an associate's or bachelor's degree? If not, why not?
- What military training courses did you take? How did you do in these courses? How are they relevant to this job?
- Did you take any correspondence courses? What were they?
- Why did you attend ____________ University (College or School)?
- Why did you major in ______________?
- What was your grade point average?
- What subjects did you enjoy the most? The least? Why?
- What leadership positions did you hold?
- How did you finance your education?
- If you started all over, what would you change about your education?
- Why were your grades so low? So high?

- Did you do the best you could in school? If not, why not?
- What plans do you have to continue your education?
- What skills do you hope to acquire through education during the next 5 years?

Work Experience

- How many different jobs have you held?
- What were your major achievements in each of your past jobs?
- What did you do in the military? Tell me about your different jobs.
- How does your military experience relate to this job?
- What did you enjoy the most about your military career? The least?
- What is your typical work day like?
- What functions do you enjoy doing the most?
- What did you like about your boss? Dislike?
- Which job did you enjoy the most/the least? Why?
- Have you ever been fired? Why?

Career Goals

- Why did you decide to leave the military?
- Why do you want to join our organization?
- Why do you think you are qualified for this position?
- Why are you looking for another job?
- Why do you want to make a career change?
- What ideally would you like to do?
- Why should we hire you?
- How would you improve our operations?
- What do you want to be doing five years from now?
- How much do you want to be making five years from now?
- What are your short-range and long-range career goals?
- If you could choose a job and organization, where would you go?
- What other jobs and companies are you considering?
- When will you be ready to begin work?
- How do you feel about relocating? Traveling? Working overtime?
- What attracted you to our organization?

Personality and Other Concerns

- Tell me about yourself.
- What are your major weaknesses? Your major strengths?
- What causes you to lose your temper?
- What do you do in your spare time? Any hobbies?
- What types of books do you read?
- What role does your family play in your career?
- How well do you work under pressure? In meeting deadlines?
- Tell me about your management philosophy.
- How much initiative do you take?
- What types of people do you prefer working with?
- How (creative, analytical, tactful, etc.) are you?
- If you could change your life, what would you do differently?

Handle Objections and Negatives With Ease

Interviewers must have a healthy skepticism of job candidates. They expect people to exaggerate their competencies and overstate what they will do for the employer. They sometimes encounter dishonest applicants, and many people they hire fail to meet their expectations. Being realists who have made poor hiring decisions before, they want to know why they should not hire you. Although they do not always ask you these questions, they think about them nonetheless:

- Why should I hire you?
- What do you really want?
- What can you really do for me?
- What are your weaknesses?
- What problems will I have with you?
- How long will you stay?

Underlying these questions are specific employers' objections to hiring you:

- You're not as good as you say you are; you probably hyped your resume.
- I'm not sure someone with military experience will fit in here.
- All you want is a job, a paycheck, and security.
- You have weaknesses like the rest of us. Is it alcohol, sex, drugs, finances, shiftlessness, petty politics?
- You'll probably want my job in another five months.
- You won't stay long with us. You'll probably join the competition or become the competition.

Some employers may have specific objections to hiring former military personnel—come from different organizational cultures, not profit-oriented, too bureaucratic, possess wrong leadership skills, or may not stay long. Employers raise such suspicions and objections because it is difficult to trust strangers in the employment game. Many have been "burned" before by excellent "role playing" applicants—those who write good resumes and perform well in the job interview but then disappoint employers on the job. Indeed, there is an alarming rise in the number of individuals lying on their resumes or falsifying their credentials.

How can you best handle employers' objections? You must first recognize their biases and stereotypes and then raise their expectations. You do this by stressing your strengths and avoiding your weaknesses. You must be impeccably honest in doing so.

Your answers to employers' questions should be positive and emphasize your strengths. Remember, the interviewer wants to know what's wrong with you—your weaknesses. When answering questions, both the substance and form of your answers should be positive. For example, such words as "couldn't," "can't," "won't," and "don't" may create a negative tone and detract from the positive and enthusiastic image you are trying to create. While you cannot eliminate all negative words, at least recognize that the type of words you use makes a difference and therefore word choice should be carefully managed. Compare your reactions to the following interview answers:

QUESTION: Why do you want to leave your present job?

ANSWER 1: After serving in the military for 20 years, I'm burned out. Morale isn't good and promotions are slow.

ANSWER 2: After serving in the military for 20 years, I've learned a great deal about leadership and teamwork. I have been given lots of responsibility for someone my age and demonstrated that I could handle it, even under high-stress situations. While I'm very proud of my military service, it's time to return to the civilian world and apply my skills and experience in that environment. I'm ready to take on more responsibilities as part of my professional growth.

Which one has the greatest impact in terms of projecting positives and strengths? The first answer communicates too many negatives. The second answer is positive and upbeat in its orientation toward skills, accomplishments, and the future.

In addition to choosing positive words, select content information which is positive and adds to the interviewer's knowledge about you. Avoid simplistic "yes/no" answers; they say nothing about you. Instead, provide information which explains your reasons and motivations behind specific events or activities. For example, how do you react to these factual answers?

QUESTION: Your background bothers me somewhat. You've been in the military over seven years. We are a profit-oriented organization. Why should I hire you?

ANSWER 1: I can understand that.

ANSWER 2: While working in the military is a service-oriented occupation, over the last few years the budget has been cut significantly and we have been forced to do "more with less." This pressure to become more cost effective has caused the military to find better and less expensive ways of doing business. I have done my part by recommending various cost-saving measures, a couple of which have been implemented. For example, in the past we discarded brass casings of spent bullets at the firing range. I recommended that we collect these casings, melt them down, and reuse them in the manufacture of new bullets. The military accepted my idea, which ultimately saved the government over $100,000 per year. If I were given the opportunity to work for your firm, I would attempt to identify analogous cost saving measures that would improve your profitability.

The first answer is incomplete. It misses an important opportunity to give evidence that you have resolved this issue in a positive manner, which is clearly reflected in the second response. The second answer provides the interviewer with a rebuttal that tactfully diffuses his assertion using a specific example.

The most difficult challenge to your positive strategy comes when the interviewer asks you to describe your negatives or weaknesses:

QUESTION: We all have our negatives and weaknesses. What are yours?

This is not the time nor situation to bluntly confess your weaknesses. But you need to provide a thoughtful and intelligent response. In so doing, you can handle this question in any of five different ways, yet still give positive information on yourself:

1. **Discuss a negative not related to the job being considered:**

   I don't enjoy accounting. I know it's important, but I find it boring. Marketing is what I like to do. Other people are much better at bookkeeping than I am. I'm glad this job doesn't involve any accounting!

2. **Discuss a negative which the interviewer already knows:**

   Since graduating from high school, I have been serving in the military. Over the last couple years, I have been taking courses leading to a bachelor's degree. As a result, I currently lack civilian work experience. However, I believe my military training and the degree I will finish this year have prepared me well for this job. My leadership experience in the military taught me how to work with people, organize, and solve problems. I write well and quickly. My research experiences helped me analyze, synthesize, and develop strategies, which were implemented by the organization.

3. **Discuss a negative which you have improved upon:**

   I used to get overcommitted and miss important deadlines. But then I read a book on time management and learned what I was doing wrong. Within three weeks I reorganized my use of time and found I could meet my deadlines with little difficulty. The quality of my work also improved. Now I have time to work out at the gym each day. I'm doing more and feeling better at the same time.

4. **Discuss a negative which can also be a positive:**

   I'm somewhat of a workaholic. Because I spend so many hours at work, I don't spend as much time with my family as I should. I'm now learning to more effectively manage my time so that I can achieve a better balance. The results to date have been positive. I've been recently recognized at work for my contributions, and my family appreciates the quality time I spend with them.

5. **Discuss a negative outside yourself:**

   I don't feel that there is anything seriously wrong with me. Like most people, I have my ups and downs. But overall I have a positive outlook, feel good about myself and what I've accomplished so far in my life. However, I am somewhat concerned how you might view my wanting to change careers. I want to assure you that I'm not making this change on a whim. I've taken my time in thinking through the issues and taking a hard look at what I do well and enjoy doing. Like a lot of young people, I guess I didn't have much life experience when I started my military career 10 years ago. However, as I got more experience and had opportunities to become a leader, my interest in management training developed. I found that I not only enjoyed those activities, but that I had some natural talent for them. While I've enjoyed my years in the military, I am committed to finding work that will enable me to build on these positive experiences.

All of these examples stress the basic point about effective interviewing. Your single best strategy for managing the interview is to emphasize your strengths and positives. Questions come in several forms. Anticipate these questions, especially the negative ones, and practice positive responses in order to project your best self in an interview situation.

Encountering Behavior-Based Interviews

More and more employers are conducting a different type of interview than they did five or ten years ago. Known as behavior-based interviews, these interviews are filled with behavior-related questions designed to elicit patterns of accomplishments relevant to the employer's situation. They challenge interviewees to provide concrete examples of their achievements in different types of situations. Such interviews are based on the simple belief that how a job candidate has responded to certain types of situations in the past is a good predictor of how that person will behave in a similar future situation. Behavior-based questions are likely to begin with some variation of:

- Give me an example of a time when you . . .
- Give me an example of how you . . .
- Tell me what you did when . . .

This is an opportunity for you to sell your positives with an example or two. Briefly describe the situation, enthusiastically explain what you did (adding information as to why) and indicate the outcome.

Obviously you want to select examples that promote your skills and have a positive outcome. Even if the interviewer asks about a time when something negative happened, try to select an example where you were able to turn the situation around and go to positive result. For example, if asked, "Tell me about a time you made a bad decision," try to identify an example where:

- Even though it wasn't the best decision, you were able to pull something positive out of the situation.

- Though it was a poor decision, you learned from it and in the next similar situation you made a good decision, or you know how you will handle it differently the next time a similar situation arises.
- It was bad decision, but the negative outcome had only minor impact.

In other words, try to pull something positive—either consequences of what you did or that you learned—out of even a negative experience you are asked to relate. As you prepare for your interview, consider situations where you:

- demonstrated leadership
- solved a problem
- increased company profits
- made a good decision/made a poor decision
- handled change or trends
- handled criticism
- met a deadline/missed a deadline
- worked as part of a team

Add to this list other behavioral questions you think of that apply to the job for which you are interviewing. For example, if the job includes making presentations, expect questions about a speech where you achieved your goal or conversely about a time when your speech failed.

Illegal Questions

Certain questions are illegal, but some employers ask them nonetheless. Consider how you would respond to these questions:

- Are you married, divorced, separated, or single?
- How old are you?
- Do you go to church regularly?
- Do you have many debts?
- Do you own or rent your home?
- What social and political organizations do you belong to?
- What does your spouse think about your career?
- Are you living with anyone?
- Are you practicing birth control?
- Were you ever arrested?
- How much insurance do you have?
- How much do you weigh?
- How tall are you?
- Do you have any disabilities?
- What child care arrangements do you have?

Don't get upset and say "That's an illegal question...I refuse to answer it!" While you may be perfectly right in saying so, this response lacks tact, which may be what the employer is looking for. For example, if you are divorced and the interviewer asks about your divorce, you might respond with "Does a divorce have a direct bearing on the responsibilities of this position?" Some employers may ask such questions just to see how you react under stress. Others may do so out of ignorance of the law. Whatever the case, be prepared to tactfully handle these questions.

Asking Questions

Interviewers expect candidates to ask intelligent, thoughtful questions concerning the organization and the nature of the work. The nature and quality of your questions reveals to the interviewer your interest in their organization and the job opening. Try to avoid asking self-centered questions that indicate you are primarily interested in knowing about salaries, benefits, perks, and advancement opportunities. Keep your questions employer- and job-centered. Consider asking some of these questions if they haven't been answered earlier in the interview:

- Please tell me about the duties and responsibilities of this job.
- How long has this position been in the organization?
- How does this position relate to other positions in the company?
- What would be the ideal type of person for this position? Skills? Personality? Working style? Background?
- Can you tell me about the people who have been in this position before?
- Backgrounds? Promotions? Terminations?
- Whom would I be working with in this position?
- Who would be my first and second level managers?
- Please tell me something about these people? Their positions? Strengths? Weaknesses? Performance expectations?
- What am I expected to accomplish during the first year?
- How will I be evaluated?
- Are promotions and raises usually tied to performance criteria?
- Are there other ways people get promoted and advance in this organization? Please tell me how this works?
- What is the normal salary range for such a position?
- Being new, what problems might I initially encounter here?
- Tell me about your experience here. What are your future plans?
- What is particularly unique about working in this organization?
- What does the future look like for this organization?

You may want to write your questions on a 3 x 5 cards and take them with you to the interview. While it is best to internalize the gist of your questions, you may need to refer to your list when the interviewer asks you if you have any questions. You might do this by saying, "Yes, I jotted down a few questions which I want to make sure I ask you before leaving." Then pull out your cards and refer to the questions. Or, better yet, ask questions that have been triggered by the interviewer's earlier comments about the company and incorporate your research-based knowledge of the company. This will have several positive effects. It will demonstrate that you are a good listener, are quick on your feet, and cared enough about the interview to take the time to learn more about a potential employer.

Dress Appropriately

Appearance is the first thing you communicate to others. Before you have a chance to speak, interviewers notice how you dress and accordingly draw certain conclusions about your personality and competence. Research shows that appearance makes the greatest difference when an evaluator has little information about the other person.

When it comes to decide what you should wear on the first interview, it depends to a significant extent on the nature of the job. For example, someone interviewing for an electrician position in a factory would wear something very different than someone else who is interviewing for a senior marketing position on Wall Street. In general, we recommend that you dress for the position. How would you know? One way is to "recon" the company a week or two before the interview—at the start of the business day—to see what others are wearing. If you know someone who works for the company, you might also ask them what they think is appropriate. Follow their advice.

If you are going to be pursing a white-collar type position, the basic attire for men or women is a suit. We recommend that you select a classic-style suit in a conservative color, such as navy blue or charcoal grey. The best suit fabrics are wool or wool blends. Under the suit we recommend that you wear a long-sleeve, white, cotton shirt with a point collar and a conservative tie.

Women's suits also should be made of a natural fiber or have the "look" of a natural fiber. For the warmer climates or the summer months, women will find few, if any, summer weight wool suits made for them. Hence linen blended with a synthetic or a good silk or silk blend are good choices.

When deciding on your professional wardrobe, always buy clothes to last, and buy quality. According to Men's Wearhouse, men should look for suit jackets that are fully lined and pants that are lined to the knee. For women, quality means buying silk blouses. Keep in mind, however, not only the price of the blouse itself, but the cleaning bill. There are many blouse fabrics that have the look and feel of silk yet are washable. Silk or a fabric that has the look and feel of silk are the fabrics for blouses to go with your suits. Choose your blouses in your most flattering shades and clarity of color. JoAnna Nicholson's two dress and image books—*Dressing Smart for Men* and *Dressing Smart for Women*—include many useful tips appropriate for interview and on-the-job success. The following books are also useful for dealing with dress and etiquette issues: *Dress Like a Big Fish; Look, Speak, and Behave for Men; Look, Speak, and Behave for Women; The Suit; Well-Dressed Gentleman's Pocket Guide; Etiquette for Dummies; and First Impressions.* Be sure to check out YouTube (www.youtube.com) clips on proper dress for job interviews by searching under these key words: dress job interview.

Appear Likable

Remember, most people invited to a job interview have already been "screened in." They supposedly possess the basic qualifications for the job, such as education and work experience. At this point employers will look for several qualities in the candidates—honesty, credibility, intelligence, competence, enthusiasm, spontaneity, friendliness, and likability. Much of the message communicating these qualities will be conveyed through your dress as well as through other nonverbal behaviors.

In the end, employers hire people they like and who will interact well on an interpersonal basis with the rest of the staff. Therefore, you should communicate that you are a likable candidate who can get along well with others. You can communicate these messages by engaging in several nonverbal behaviors. Four of the most important ones include:

1. **Sit with a very slight forward lean toward the interviewer.** It should be so slight as to be almost imperceptible. If not overdone, it communicates your interest in what the interviewer is saying.
2. **Make eye contact frequently, but don't overdo it.** Good eye contact establishes rapport with the interviewer. You will be perceived as more trustworthy if you will look at the interviewer as you ask and answer questions.
3. **A moderate amount of smiling will also help reinforce your positive image.** You should smile enough to convey your positive attitude, but not so much that you will not be taken seriously. Some people naturally smile often and others hardly ever smile. Monitor your behavior or ask a friend to give you feedback.
4. **Try to convey interest and enthusiasm through your vocal inflections.** Your tone of voice can say a lot about you and how interested you are in the interviewer and organization.

Close the Interview

Be prepared to end the interview. Many people don't know when or how to close interviews. They go on and on until someone breaks an uneasy moment of silence with an indication that it is time to go.

Interviewers normally will initiate the close by standing, shaking hands, and thanking you for coming to the interview. Don't end by saying "Good-bye and thank you." You should summarize the interview in terms of your interests, strengths, and goals. Briefly restate your qualifications and continued interest in working with the employer. At this point it is proper to ask the interviewer about selection plans: "*When do you anticipate making your final decision?*"

Follow this question with your final one: "*May I call you next week (or whatever is appropriate in response to your question about timing of the final decision) to inquire about my status?*"

By taking the initiative in this manner, the employer will be prompted to clarify your status soon, and you will have an opportunity to talk to him/her further.

Many interviewers will ask you for a list of references. Be sure to prepare such a list prior to the interview. Include the names, addresses, and phone numbers of four individuals who will give you positive professional and personal recommendations.

Remember to Follow Up

Once you have been interviewed, be sure to follow through to get nearer to the job offer. One of the best follow-up methods is the thank-you letter; you will find examples of these letters at the end of Chapter 7. After talking to the employer over the telephone or in a face-to-face interview, send a thank-you letter. This letter should be typed on good quality bond paper. In this letter express your gratitude for the opportunity to interview. Restate your interest in the position and highlight any particularly noteworthy points made in your conversation or anything you wish to further clarify. Close the letter by mentioning that you will call in a few days to inquire about the employer's decision. When you do this, the employer should remember you as a thoughtful person.

If you call and the employer has not yet made a decision, follow through with another phone call in a few days. Send any additional information to the employer which may enhance your application. It's fine to send an updated resume that better orients your skills and experience to what you have learned is most important to this company and the job that you are pursuing. You might also want to ask one of your references to call the employer to further recommend you for the position. However, don't engage in overkill by making a pest of yourself. You want to tactfully communicate two things to the employer at this point: (1) you are interested in the job, and (2) you will do a good job.

A good way to keep track of your interviews is to maintain a record of each interview, such as with an Excel spreadsheet. You might include columns such as Company Name, Interviewer's Name, Interviewer's Phone Number, Interviewer's Email Address, Date of Interview, Interview Outcome, Next Steps, etc.

For more information and exercises to help you interview like a pro, visit www.CorporateGray.com and click on the Transition Guide tab.

chapter 12

Negotiate Salary and Benefits

THROUGHOUT YOUR JOB SEARCH you need to seriously consider several questions about your financial value and future income. What, for example, are you worth to a prospective employer? How do you know? What is the equivalent value of your total military compensation in civilian pay? How much should you be paid for your work? How can you demonstrate your value to an employer? What dollar value will employers assign to you? What are you willing to accept? How much do you need to make to maintain your family's lifestyle now? After retirement?

For most people transitioning from the military, these are difficult questions that require considerable thought and research. Since your entry on active duty, you've been accustomed to well-defined pay scales that dictate how much you'll be paid based on your pay grade, years of service, and marital status. That situation is about to change dramatically. After impressing upon a prospective employer that you are the right person for the job, the bottom line becomes money—your talent and labor in exchange for the employer's cash and benefits. How, then, will you deal with these questions in order to get more than employers initially offer?

You may think you are worth a lot in the civilian work world—more than you have been getting paid in the military. But when it comes to questions of compensation, you must go beyond wishful thinking. As we will see in this chapter, you need to know how to value both the job and your skills and then translate these values into specific dollar figures.

Approach Salaries as Negotiable

As you know, your military salary has been set by the government based on your rank and years of service. The situation is far different in the private sector. You must be prepared to negotiate your compensation based on your projected value to the employer. Once you are employed, your job performance becomes the key driver in terms of compensation.

Salary is one of the most important yet least understood considerations in the job search. Many individuals do well in handling all interview questions except the salary question. They are either too shy to talk about money or believe they must take what is offered—because salary is predetermined by employers. As a result, many applicants may be paid much less than they are worth. Over the years, they will lose thousands of dollars by having failed to properly negotiate their salaries.

Salary is seldom predetermined. Most employers have some flexibility to negotiate salary. While most employers do not try to exploit applicants, neither do they want to pay applicants more than what they are willing to accept.

Salaries are usually assigned to positions or jobs rather than to individuals. But not everyone is of equal value in performing the job; some are more productive than others. Since individual performance differs, you should attempt to establish your value in the eyes of the employer rather than accept a salary figure for the job. The art of salary negotiation will help you do this.

Look to Your Financial Future

> The salary you receive today will influence your future earnings.

We all have financial needs which our salary helps to meet. But salary has other significance too. It is an indicator of our worth to others. It also influences our future income. Therefore, it should be treated as one of the most serious considerations in the job interview.

The salary you receive today will influence your future earnings. Yearly salary increments will most likely be figured as a percentage of your base salary rather than reflect your actual job performance. Expect employers to offer you a salary similar to the one you earned in your last job. Once they learn what you made in your previous job, they will probably offer you no more than a 10% to 15% increase. If you hope to improve your income in the long run, then you must be willing to negotiate your salary from a position of strength.

Military Pay and Civilian Salary Parity

Many transitioning service members often undervalue themselves in the civilian work world because they tend to equate salary with base pay. If you've received base housing or a housing allowance, you know this benefit can be considerable. It translates into a specific dollar figure which should be added to your base salary. For example, if your base pay as an NCO is $60,000 a year, you should include another 20 percent in benefits to arrive at a total compensation figure that would be equivalent to a civilian salary—around $72,000. Commissioned officers making $80,000 a year in base pay should figure their total compensation to be approximately $96,000. If you only use your base pay as your current salary figure, you may undervalue yourself to civilian employers. For those of you receiving "professional pay" or additional money for living in a hardship area, don't forget to include this in your total compensation computations.

To determine your equivalent civilian compensation, visit:

http://militarypay.defense.gov/pay/calc

Prepare for the Salary Question

You should be well prepared to deal with the question of salary anytime during your job search but especially during the job interview. Based on your research (Chapter 9) and networking activities (Chapter 10), you should know the approximate salary range for the position you are seeking. Another increasingly popular source of information regarding salary is the Web. There are several Internet websites that will be of interest, including:

- **Online salary surveys and employment sites:** Several websites include salary information. Among the most useful are www.Salary.com, www.SalaryScout.com, www.SalaryExpert.com, www.jobnob.com, www.PayScale.com, www.GlassDoor.com, www.SimplyHired.com, www.indeed.com, www.cbsalary.com, and www. Vault.com. Many online employment sites, such as www.monster.com and http://online.wsj.com/careers, include salary survey information as well as salary ranges for specific positions.
- **Trade and professional associations:** Most associations conduct annual salary surveys of their members. Contact them for the latest information on salary ranges. The best print reference for identifying these associations is the *Encyclopedia of Associations*; on the Web at http://library.dialog.com/bluesheets/html/bl0114.html.
- **Newspapers and print media:** Many of the larger newspapers now provide online access to their classified section, which contains listings of job openings. By visiting Editor and Publisher Interactive (www.editorandpublisher.com) you'll be able to quickly traverse your way to more than 600 electronic newspapers and their classified job listings.

If you fail to gather this salary information prior to the screening or job interview, you may do yourself a disservice by accepting too low a figure or pricing yourself out of consideration. By being informed, you will be in better control to negotiate salary and benefits.

Keep Salary Issues to the Very End

The question of salary may be raised anytime during the job search. Employers may want you to state a salary expectation figure on an application form, in a cover letter, or over the telephone. Most frequently, however, employers will talk about salary during the employment interview. If at all possible, keep the salary question open until the very last, and remember, you always talk about your TOTAL military compensation rather than your base pay. Even with application forms, cover letters, and telephone screening interviews, try to delay the discussion of salary by stating "open" or "negotiable." After all, the ultimate purpose of your job search activities is to demonstrate your value to employers. You should not attempt to translate your value into dollar figures until you have had a chance to convince the employer of your worth. This is best done near the end of the job interview.

Although employers will have a salary figure or range in mind when they interview you, they still want to know your salary expectations. How much will you cost them? Will it be more or less than the job is worth? Employers preferably want to hire individuals for the least amount possible. You, on the other hand, want to be hired for as much as possible. Obviously, there is room for disagreement and unhappiness as well as negotiation and compromise.

One easy way employers screen you in or out of consideration is to raise the salary question early in the interview. A standard question is: "What are your salary requirements?" When asked, don't answer with a specific dollar figure. You should aim at establishing your value in the eyes of the employer prior to talking about a figure. If you give the employer a salary figure at this stage, you are likely to lock yourself into it, regardless of how much you impress the employer or what you find out about the duties and responsibilities of the job. Therefore, salary should be the last major item you discuss with the employer.

You should never ask about salary prior to being offered the job. Let the employer initiate the salary question. And when he or she does, take your time. While you may know —based on your previous research—approximately what the employer will offer, try to get the employer to state a figure first. If you do this, you will be in a stronger negotiating position.

Handle the Salary Question With Tact

When the salary question arises, assuming you cannot or do not want to put it off until later, your first step should be to clearly summarize the job responsibilities/duties as you understand them. At this point you are attempting to do three things:

1. Seek clarification from the interviewer as to the actual job and all it involves.
2. Emphasize the level of skills required in the most positive way. In other words, you emphasize the value and worth of this position to the organization. This may help support the actual figure that the interviewer or you later provide.
3. Focus attention on your value in relation to the requirements of the position—the critical linkage for negotiating salary from a position of strength.

You might do this, for example, by saying:

> *As I understand it, I would report directly to the vice-president in charge of marketing and I would have full authority for marketing decisions that involved expenditures of up to $50,000. I would have a staff of five people—an administrative assistant, two copywriters, and two marketing assistants.*

Such a summary statement establishes for both you and the interviewer that (1) this position reports to the highest levels of authority; (2) this position is responsible for decision-making involving fairly large sums of money; and (3) this position involves supervision of staff.

Although you may not explicitly draw the connection, you are emphasizing the value of this position to the organization. This position should be worth a lot more than one in which the hiree will report to the marketing manager, be required to get approval for all expenditures over $100, and has no staff—just access to the secretarial pool! By doing this you will focus the salary question (which you have not yet responded to) around the exact work you must perform on the job in exchange for salary and benefits. You have also seized the opportunity to focus on the value of the person who will be selected to fill this vacancy.

Your conversation might go something like this. The employer poses the question:

> *What are your salary requirements?*

Your first response should be to summarize the responsibilities of the position. You might begin with a summary statement followed by a question:

> *Let me see if I understand all that is involved with this position and job. I would be expected to ___________. Have I covered everything or are there some other responsibilities I should know about?*

This response focuses the salary question around the value of the position in relation to you. After the interviewer responds to your final question, answer the initial salary expectation question in this manner:

> *What is your normal salary range for a position such as this?*

This question establishes the value as well as the range for the position or job—two important pieces of information you need before proceeding further into the salary negotiation stage. The employer normally will give you the requested salary range. Once he or she does, depending on how you feel about the figure, you can follow up with one more question.

What would be the normal salary range for someone with my qualifications?

This question further establishes the value for the individual versus the position. This line of questioning will yield the salary expectations of the employer without revealing your desired salary figure or range. It also will indicate whether the employer distinguishes between individuals and positions when establishing salary figures.

Reach Common Ground and Agreement

After finding out what the employer is prepared to offer, you have several choices. First, you can indicate that his or her figure is acceptable to you and thus conclude your final interview. Second, you can negotiate for more money in the hope of reaching an acceptable compromise. Third, you can delay final action by asking for more time to consider the figure. Finally, you can tell the employer the figure is unacceptable and leave.

The first and the last options indicate you are either too eager or playing hard-to-get. We recommend the second and third options. If you decide to reach agreement on salary in this interview, negotiate in a professional manner. You can do this best by establishing a salary range from which to bargain in relation to the employer's salary range. For example, if the employer indicates that he or she is prepared to offer $40,000 to $45,000, you should establish common ground for negotiation by placing your salary range into the employer's range. Your response to the employer's $40,000 to $45,000 range might be:

Yes, that does come near what I was expecting. I was thinking more in terms of $45,000 to $50,000.

You, in effect, place the top of the employer's range into the bottom of your range. At this point you may be able to negotiate a salary of $42,000 to $43,000, depending on how much flexibility the employer has with salaries. Most employers have more flexibility than they admit.

Once you have placed your expectations at the top of the employer's salary range, you need to emphasize your value with supports, such as examples, illustrations, descriptions, definitions, statistics, comparisons, or testimonials. It is not enough to simply state you were "thinking" in a certain range; you must state why you believe you are worth what you want. Using statistics and comparisons as your supports, you might say, for example:

The salary surveys I have studied indicate that for the position of ________ in this industry and region the salary is between $65,000 and $70,000. Since, as we have discussed, I have extensive experience in all the areas you outlined, I would not need training in the job duties themselves—just a brief orientation to the operating procedures you use here at ________ . I'm sure I could be up and running in this job within a week or two. Taking everything in consideration—especially my skills and experience and what I see as my future contributions here—I really feel a salary of $70,000 is fair compensation. Is this possible here at ____________?

Another option is to ask the employer for time to think about the salary offer. You want to sleep on it for a day or two. A common professional courtesy is to give you at least 48 hours to consider an offer. During this time, you may want to carefully examine the job. Is it worth what you are being offered? Can you do better? What are other employers offering for comparable positions? If one or two other employers are considering you for a job, let this employer know his or her job is not the only one under consideration.

Let the employer know you may be in demand elsewhere. This should give you a better bargaining position. Contact the other employers and let them know you have a job offer and that you would like to have your application status with them clarified before you make any decisions with the other employer. Depending on how much flexibility an employer may have to accelerate a hiring decision, you may be able to go back to the first employer with another job offer. With a second job offer in hand, you should greatly enhance your bargaining position.

In both recommended options, you need to keep in mind that you should always negotiate from a position of knowledge and strength—not because of need or greed. Learn about salaries for your occupation, establish your value, discover what the employer is willing to pay, and negotiate in a professional manner. How you negotiate your salary will affect your future relations with the employer. In general, applicants who negotiate well will be treated well on the job.

Carefully Examine Benefits

You should make sure your future salary reflects your value.

While serving in the military, you may have taken certain benefits, such as medical care, life insurance, and even physical fitness centers, for granted. In the civilian work world, these items and others like them have a direct cost that is carefully managed by employers. Given that the range of benefits may vary considerably from one company to the next, we recommend that you take these benefits into account when evaluating your job offers.

Most companies will include some type of retirement savings plan (usually a 401k), medical insurance (you will likely pay for part of this), life insurance, short-term disability insurance, and paid holidays and vacations (generally two weeks for starters; increases with longevity in the company). Other benefits, such as bonuses and stock options, are normally reserved for those individuals entering the firm at the executive level. Many start-up companies also offer their initial employees stock options as compensation for lower-than-standard salaries. In general, you can expect that mature companies have a standard suite of benefits and there will be little room for negotiation. Some of the smaller companies, however, might be willing to negotiate over benefits.

Offer a Renegotiation Option

You should make sure your future salary reflects your value. One approach to doing this is to reach an agreement to renegotiate your salary at a later date, perhaps in another six months. Use this technique especially when you feel the final salary offer is less than what you are worth, but you want to accept the job. Employers often will agree to this provision since they have nothing to lose and much to gain if you are as productive as you tell them.

Renegotiation provisions stress one very important point—you want to be paid on the basis of your performance. You demonstrate your professionalism, self-confidence, and competence by negotiating in this manner. More importantly, you ensure that the question of your monetary value will not be closed in the future. As you negotiate the present, you also negotiate your future with this as well as other employers.

Take Time Before Accepting

You should accept an offer only after reaching a salary agreement. If you jump at an offer, you may appear needy. Take time to consider your options. Remember, you are committing your time and effort in exchange for money and status. Is this the job you really want?

Take some time to think about the offer before giving the employer a definite answer. But don't play hard-to-get and thereby create ill will with your new employer.

While considering the offer, ask yourself several of the same questions you asked at the beginning of your job search:

- What do I want to be doing five years from now?
- How will this job affect my personal life?
- Am I willing to travel? How many days per week/month?
- Do I know enough about the employer and this organization?
- How have previous occupants of this position fared? Why did they have problems?
- Are there other jobs I'm considering which would better meet my goals?

Accepting a job is serious business. If you make a mistake, you could be locked into a very unhappy situation for a long time.

If you receive one job offer while considering another, you will be able to compare relative advantages and disadvantages. You also will have some external leverage for negotiating salary and benefits. While you should not play games, let the employer know you have alternative job offers. This communicates that you are in demand, others also know your value, and the employer's price is not the only one in town. Use this leverage to negotiate your salary, benefits, and job responsibilities.

If you get a job offer but you are considering other employers, let the others know you have a job offer. Telephone them to inquire about your status as well as inform them of the job offer. Sometimes this will prompt employers to make a hiring decision sooner than anticipated. In addition you will be letting them that you are in demand; they should seriously consider you before you get away!

Some job seekers play a bluffing game by telling employers they have alternative job offers even though they don't. Some candidates do this and get away with it. We don't recommend this approach. Not only is it dishonest, it will work to your disadvantage if the employer learns that you were lying. But more importantly, you should be selling yourself on the basis of your strengths rather than your deceit and greed. If you can't sell yourself honestly, don't expect to get along well on the job. When you compromise your integrity, you demean your value.

Your job search is not over with the job offer and acceptance. You need to set the stage for launching a successful career with your new employer. Be thoughtful by sending your new employer a nice thank-you letter. As outlined at the end of Chapter 7, this is one of the most effective letters to write for getting your new job off on the right foot. The employer will remember you as a thoughtful individual and will look forward to working with you. The whole point of our job search methods is to clearly communicate to employers that you are competent and worthy of your salary. If you follow our advice, you should do well in your salary negotiations.

Translate Your Value Into Productivity for Others

One final word of advice. Many job seekers have unrealistic salary expectations and exaggerated notions of their worth to potential employers. Given the increased emphasis on productivity and performance in the workplace, many employers are reluctant to negotiate salaries upwards prior to seeing you perform in their organization. Because of this, you may find it difficult to negotiate salaries with employers. You will need to stress your value more than ever. For example, if you think you are worth $60,000 a year in salary, will you be productive enough to generate enough business for the company to justify that amount? Make sure you can translate your salary expectations into dollars and cents profits for the employer!

Evaluating Multiple Job Offers

Scores: 1 = Poor; 2 = Below Average; 3 = Average; Above Average = 4; Excellent = 5

Job #1: ______________________________ (Job Title, Company)

Score

Evaluation Factor	**1**	**2**	**3**	**4**	**5**
Nature of Work					
Advancement Opportunity					
Training					
Work Environment					
Direct Supervisor					
Co-Workers					
Location					
Commute Time					
Salary					
Benefits (health care, insurance, etc.)					
Subtotal					
Total					

For a helpful Job Offer Evaluation form and more information to help you negotiate your best salary, visit www.CorporateGray.com and click on the Transition Guide tab.

chapter 13

Implement Your Goals

UNDERSTANDING WITHOUT ACTION is a waste of time. Many people read how-to books, attend how-to seminars, and do nothing other than read more books, attend more seminars, and engage in more wishful thinking. While these activities become forms of therapy for some individuals, they should lead to positive actions for you. After all, as a servicemember you are used to developing and implementing plans in order to achieve assigned objectives.

You Are the Magic Pill

From the very beginning of this book we have stressed the importance of understanding the job market, developing an appropriate job search strategy, and implementing a well thought out plan to obtain the job you seek. We said then and we say now, there are no magic pills to make your quest for the right job successful. However, we are confident that you will find success if you follow the guidance we have prescribed. We have attempted to assemble useful information to help you organize and implement an effective job search. Individual chapters examined the present and future job markets as well as outlined in how-to terms specific job search skills for shaping your own future. We have done our part in getting you to the implementation stage. What happens next is your responsibility.

The methods we outlined in previous chapters have worked for many former military personnel who have successfully made their transition from the military to the civilian work world. We are confident that you will soon follow in their footsteps. But along the way, you may experience rejection as you seek to find the job that is right for you. As we've said previously, changing careers is an ego-sensitive activity. Therefore, it's important to have support structures in place to help you if necessary. Through the career transition programs discussed in Chapter 3, you can obtain the professional services of some outstanding career counselors. They understand that changing careers is difficult and takes work. It's their job to help you succeed. Give them a chance.

Welcome Rejections as Learning Opportunities

Planning is the easiest part of any task. Turning plans into reality is the most difficult challenge. It's relatively simple to set goals and outline a course of action divorced from the reality of actually doing it. But if you don't take action, you will not get your expected results. You must implement if you want desired results.

> Rejections offer an important learning experience.

Once you take action, be prepared for rejections. Employers will tell you, "Thank you—we'll call you," but they never do. Other employers will tell you, "We have no positions available at this time for someone with your qualifications" or "You don't have the qualifications necessary for this position." Whatever the story, you will face many disappointments on the road to success.

Rejections are a normal part of the process of finding employment as well as getting ahead in life. Rejections offer an important learning experience which should help you better understand yourself, employers, and the job finding process. Expect 10 rejections or "nos" for every acceptance. If you quit after five or eight rejections, you prematurely end your job search. If you persist in collecting two to five more "nos," you will likely receive a "yes." Most people quit prematurely because their ego is not prepared for more rejections. Therefore, you should welcome rejections as you seek more and more acceptances.

Get Motivated and Work Hard

Assuming you have a firm understanding of each job search step and how to relate them to your goals, what do you do next? The next steps involve motivation and hard work. Just how motivated are you to seek a new job or career and thus your life? Our experience is that individuals need to be sufficiently motivated to make the first move and do it properly. If you go about your job search halfheartedly—you just want to "test the waters" to see what's out there—don't expect to be successful. You must be committed to achieving specific goals. Make the decision to properly develop and implement your job search and be prepared to work hard in achieving your goals.

Find Time

Once you've convinced yourself to take the necessary steps to find a job or change and advance your career, you need to find the time to properly implement your job search. This requires setting aside specific blocks of time for identifying your motivated abilities and skills, developing your resume, writing letters, making telephone calls, and conducting the necessary research and networking required for success. This whole process takes time. If you are a busy person, like most people, you simply must make the time. As noted in our examination of your time management practices in Chapter 2, you should practice your own versions of time management or cut-back management. Get better organized, give some things up, or cut back on all your activities. If, for example, you can set aside one hour each day to devote to your job search, you will spend seven hours a week or 28 hours a month on your search. However, you should and can find more time than this.

Time and again we find successful job hunters are the ones who routinize a job search schedule and keep at it. They make contact after contact, conduct numerous informational interviews, submit many applications and resumes, and keep repeating these activities in spite of encountering rejections. They learn that success is just a few more "no's" and informational interviews away. They face each day with a positive attitude.

Commit Yourself in Writing

You may find it useful to commit yourself in writing to achieving job search success. This is a very useful way to get both motivated and directed for action. Start by completing a job search contract, which appears on the next page, and keep it near you—in your briefcase or on your desk. In addition, you should complete weekly performance reports. These reports identify what you actually accomplished rather than what your good intentions tell you to do. Use these reports to track your actual progress and to plan your activities for the next week.

If you fail to meet these written commitments, issue yourself a revised and updated contract. But if you do this three or more times, we strongly suggest that you question your motivation and commitment to find a job. Start over again, but this time consult a professional career counselor who can provide you with a structure for making progress in finding a job.

A professional may not be cheap, but if paying for help gets you on the right track and results in the job you want, it's money well spent. Do not be "penny wise but pound foolish" with your future. If you must seek professional advice, be sure you are an informed consumer according to our "shopping" advice in Chapter 2.

Change Careers for Securing Your Future

If you want to make the very best career change possible, you should be prepared to develop and practice our careering competencies in the decade ahead. We recommend two final career actions on your part. First, make an effort to learn one new skill each year; the skill can be related to work, family, community, or a hobby such as building bookcases, operating different computer software programs, repairing appliances, or remodeling your home. If you do this, you will be better prepared for making the career transitions necessary for functioning effectively in turbulent times.

Second, develop your own five-year plan which incorporates yearly career check-ups. At the end of each year, ask yourself: To what degree have I achieved my goals? Which goals do I need to revise? What actions do I need to take to better achieve my goals?

Jobs and careers should not be viewed as life sentences. You should feel free to change jobs and careers when you want to or need to. In fact, thousands of people make successful career transitions each year. Some are more successful than others in finding the right job. If you plan your career transition according to the methods outlined in previous chapters, you should be able to successfully land the job you want.

Jobs and careers should not be viewed as life sentences.

Treat yourself right. Take the time and effort to sail into today's job market with a plan of action that links your qualifications to the needs of employers. You are first and foremost an individual with knowledge, abilities, and skills that many employers need and want. If you follow the advice of this book, you will put your best foot forward in communicating your qualifications to employers. You will find a job fit for you and a career that is both satisfying and rewarding. You'll discover your best years still lie ahead as you pursue your new career.

Job Search Contract

1. I'm committed to changing my life by changing my job. Today's date is ______ ____________________________.

2. I will manage my time so that I can successfully complete my job search and find a high quality job. I will begin changing my time management behavior on ____________________________.

3. I will begin my job search on ____________________________.

4. I will involve ____________________________ with my job search.
   (individual/group)

5. I will spend at least one week conducting library and Internet research on different jobs, employers, and organizations. I will begin this research during the week of____________________________.

6. I will complete my skills identification step by____________________.

7. I will complete my objective statement by ____________________.

8. I will complete my resume by ____________________________.

9. Each week I will:
   - make ________ new job contacts.
   - conduct ________ informational interviews.
   - follow up on ________ referrals.

10. My first job interview will take place during the week of ____________________________.

11. I will begin my new job by ____ ____ ____

12. I will make a habit of learning one new skill each year.

Signature: ____

Date: ____